CW00349352

Edinburgh

MICHELIN
Travel Publications

CONTENTS

Introduction	5
Geography	7
History	8
People and culture	15
Scottish specialities	22
Main Sights	25
Edinburgh Castle	26
Holyroodhouse	34
Royal Mile	38
South of the Royal Mile	46
University Campus	48
New Town	54
Princes Street and Gardens	60
Calton Hill	66
Northern and Western Edinburgh	68
Southern Suburbs	74
Practical Information	77
Planning a Trip	78
Getting there	78
Sightseeing	80
Shopping	81
Entertainment	81
Where to Stay and Where to Eat	83
Further Reading	87
Calendar of Events	88
Index	90

INTRODUCTION

" There are no stars so lovely as Edinburgh street lamps," wrote Robert Louis Stevenson and, whichever way and whatever time of day you view her, Edinburgh is one of Europe's most beautiful cities. There's not another capital which has a green swathe like Princes Street Gardens running through its heart, nor one that has a mini mountain like Arthur's Seat right in the city centre; no other capital has so many panoramic viewpoints or quirky ups and downs. Her crag-top castle is the stuff of fairy tales, while the dark narrow alleyways of the Old Town and higgledy-piggledy buildings along its half-hidden closes and alleyways (wynds) are straight out of a period film set.

By contrast, down in the New Town all is harmony and light. Only in Dublin and Bath will you see such splendid Georgian terraces and well-ordered circuses, while out in the suburbs are neat and characterful villages and unspoiled hills and countryside.

Modern day Edinburgh is neither the tartan-shortbread theme park of Sir Walter Scott, nor so steeped in its own history that its future is stifled. Its many students and festivals ensure that it remains a vibrant young city, and its banking and service industries are in good shape. Now, with a modern Parliament in residence and so much going on for locals and visitors, the future for Edinburgh looks bright.

Richard CAMPBELL/AZB

■ Geography

Edinburgh lies some 20mi/32km inland from the east coast of Scotland and 55mi/88km north of the border with England. The city centre is less than 2mi/3km south of the broad estuary known as the Firth of Forth, and its port Leith. The Forth is visible from any vantage point in the Old Town, and on clear days makes a wonderful backdrop to the city. Like Rome, Edinburgh is built on seven hills, though it may seem many more as you puff your way up and down. Three of these – Castle Rock, Arthur's Seat and Calton Hill – are right in the centre: the others – Corstophine Hill (home to the zoo), Blaxkford Hill (home to the Royal Observatory), Braid Hill and Wester Craiglockheart – are just a few minutes' bus ride away. The highest at 823ft/251m is Arthur's Seat, like Castle Hill, an ancient volcanic plug. The smallest, at 328ft/100m, is Calton Hill. The views from all are well worth the climb. The hilly, undulating nature of Edinburgh city centre and the viewpoints offered from all sorts of different angles and heights are what make it so interesting and picturesque. Linking one part of the city to the next are hundreds of steps and some spectacular bridges. This is one of the world's finest cities for walking, so make sure you bring comfortable shoes.

One o'clock gun at
Edinburgh Castle

■ History

The Castle Rock no doubt proved to be a secure refuge for the earliest settlers, although the Romans preferred the attractions of Cramond. The name may in fact be derived from the Northumbrian King Edwin (Edwinesburg – Edwin's fortress) although he actually died before his people captured the site in 638. As a residence, the Castle Rock site was associated with **Malcolm Canmore** and his **Queen Margaret**. Their son **David I** gave great preferment to the settlement by founding the Abbey of Holy Rood and the building of a small chapel to commemorate his mother. During the Wars of Independence, the strategic importance of the castle not only afforded protection to the growing burgh but also made it more susceptible to English attacks.

Medieval Golden Age

The first town wall dated from 1450. With the early Stewarts, Edinburgh slowly assumed the roles of royal residence, seat of government and capital. Already an important religious centre with the abbey and St Giles', 15C Edinburgh gained two collegiate churches, Kirk o'Field (1450) outside the wall and Holy Trinity (1462), which stood on the site of Waverley Station. Court patronage included the foundation of a College of Surgeons (1505) and the introduction of printing (1507). Some of the earliest works printed were those of the court poet William Dunbar (1460-1520) and of Gavin Douglas (1475-1522) both of whom used vernacular to good effect, and belonged to a group of poets known as the Makars.

This Golden Age ended with Flodden *(see Index)* when the host of Scots dead included the king and Edinburgh's provost. In haste the town started to build the **Flodden Wall**; although only completed in 1560 this was to define the limits of the Ancient Royalty for over two centuries confining expansion upwards in the characteristic lands (tenements) of as many as 10 and 12 storeys.

Mary, Queen of Scots and the Reformation

Two years after the proclamation of the infant Mary's accession, Henry VIII's army set out on the **"rough wooing"**, creating havoc and destruction in the south and east of the country. Mary was sent to France for safety. Already the Roman Catholic church, wealthier than the Crown, was under attack and the ideas of the Reformation gained ground. The **Reformation** (1560) and the return of the Catholic Mary, Queen of Scots, a year later, made Edinburgh, during her short reign, the stage for warring factions, Protestant and

Roman Catholic, pro-French and pro-English. Renewed patronage of the arts came with the reign of Mary's son, James VI. With the departure of James and his court after the **Union of the Crowns** (1603), some citizens prospered in the south like "Jinglin Geordie" *(see George Heriot's School)*, but Edinburgh lost much of its pageantry and cultural activity.

Religious strife

Relative peace ensued until Charles I, following his 1633 coronation at Holyrood, pushed through Episcopacy (government of the church by bishops) – a policy inherited from his father. **The National Covenant** was drawn up in 1638 and signed in Greyfriars Church. The signatories swore loyalty to the King but fervently opposed his religious policy. A year later, following the General Assembly of Glasgow, episcopacy was abolished. Covenanters took the castle. By 1641 Charles had conceded to the Covenanters (defendants of the Reformed Faith) but the outbreak of the English Civil War brought a pact with the English Parliamentarians, the **Solemn League and Covenant** (1643). The brilliant royalist campaign led by the Marquess of Montrose *(see Index)* ended with defeat at Philliphaugh (1645) and the final outcome of the Parliamentary victory at Marston Moor near York was the king's execution (1649).

Cromwell defeated the Scots at Dunbar (1650) and Montrose was executed. His troops entered Edinburgh and the palace and other buildings served as barracks, some like Holyroodhouse suffered through fire. The Commonwealth was a period of uneasy peace in Edinburgh and much was the rejoicing at the Restoration in spite of the fact that it brought the reintroduction of the episcopal system and persecution of the Covenanters. Slowly the Covenanting opposition was eradicated. Many of the prisoners were either executed in the Grassmarket or kept prisoner in Greyfriars Churchyard *(see Index)*.

In the late 17C Edinburgh flourished as a legal and medical centre. The failure of the Darien scheme – its aims were to promote Scottish overseas trade and to control trade between the Atlantic and the Pacific – gave rise to anti-English feelings which were exacerbated by the Union Debates. The activities of both factions were closely followed by Daniel Defoe in his role of government spy. In 1707 Edinburgh lost its Parliament when the politicians headed south. The legal profession took over Parliament Hall and began to dominate Edinburgh society.

Of the two Jacobite rebellions, that of 1745 saw the return of a brief period of glory to Holyroodhouse with the installation of the prin-

Abbey and Palace
  of Holyroodhouse......**BY**
Adam Theatre................**BZ T¹**
Appleton Tower.............**BZ U¹**
Assembly Rooms...........**AY**
Baillie Mac Morran's
  House..........................**BYZ A**
Brass Rubbing Centre..**BY B**
Buchan House................**BY**
Café Royal....................**BY D**
Calton Hill....................**BY**
Canongate Church.......**BY**
Canongate Tolbooth.....**BY**
Castle............................**AZ**
Castle Esplanade...........**BZ**
Church of Scotland General
  Assembly Hall..............**BY F**
Circular Greek
  Temple........................**BY G**
City Chambers...............**BY H**
Committee Chambers...**BY K¹**
David Hume Tower.......**BZ U²**
Dundas House...............**BY**
East Meadow Park........**BZ**
East Princes Street
  Gardens......................**BY**
Festival Theatre...........**BZ T²**
Flodden Wall.................**BZ**
Floral clock...................**BY K²**
General Register
  House..........................**BY K³**
George Heriot's
  School..........................**BZ**
Georgian House.............**AY**
Gladstone's Land...........**BY**
Greek Temple...............**BY K⁴**
Greyfriars Church.........**BZ**
Heriot Watt
  University....................**BZ J**
James Craig
  Observatory.................**BY K⁶**
John Knox House.........**BY L¹**
Lady Stair's House.......**BY M²**
Library..........................**BZ U³**
McEwan Hall................**BZ U⁵**
Medical School..............**BZ U⁶**
Moray House.................**BY L²**
Mowbray House............**BY L⁴**
Museum of Childhood..**BY M⁴**
Museum of Edinburgh..**BY M¹**

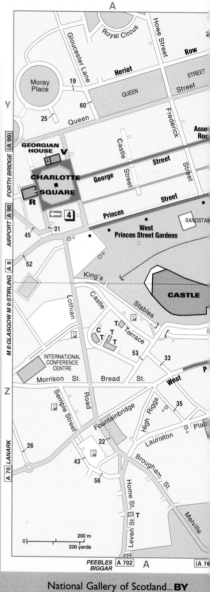

National Gallery of Scotland...**BY**
National Monument.....................**BY**
Nelson's Monument.....................**BY**
New Register House.....................**BY N**
Old Post Office.............................**BY**

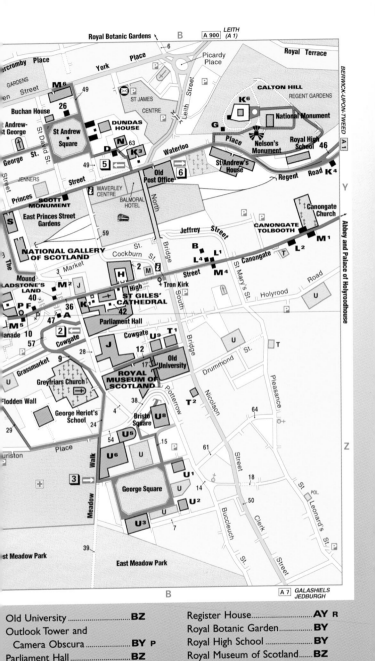

Old University	**BZ**
Outlook Tower and Camera Obscura	**BY P**
Parliament Hall	**BZ**
Ramsay Lodge	**BY Q**
Register House	**AY R**
Royal Botanic Garden	**BY**
Royal High School	**BY**
Royal Museum of Scotland	**BZ**
Royal Scottish Academy	**BY S**

Scotch Whisky Heritage
  Centre............................**BZ** M[5]
Scott Monument........................**BY**
Scottish National Portrait
  Gallery........................**BY** M[6]
St Andrew's House....................**BY**
St Andrew-St George................**BY**

St Giles Cathedral ....**BY**
Student Centre............................**BZ** U[8]
Tron Kirk.....................................**BY**
University Staff Club....................**BZ** U[9]
West Meadow Park ....**BZ**
West Princes Street Gardens ..**AY**
5-7 Charlotte Square ....**AY** v

Abercromby Pl. .... BY
Anchor Close................................ BY 2
Bank St... AZ 3
Bread St....................................... AZ
Bristo Pl....................................... BZ 4
Bristo Square............................... BZ
Brougham St................................ AZ
Broughton St............................... BY 6
Buccleuch Pl................................. BZ 7
Buccleuch St................................ BZ
Candlemaker Row......................... BZ 9
Canongate.................................... BY
Castle Hill .... BYZ 10
Castle St....................................... AY
Castle Terrace .... AZ
Chalmers St .... BZ
Chambers St................................. BZ 12
Chapel St...................................... CZ 14
Charles St..................................... BZ 15
Charlotte Square.......................... AY
Clerk St... BZ
Cockburn St .... BY
College St .... BZ 17
Cowgate.. BZ
Cross Causeway .... CZ 18
Darneway St .... AY 19
Drummond St............................... BZ
Dundas St...................................... AY 21
Earl Grey St .... AZ 22
Forest Rd .... BZ 24
Forres St....................................... AY 25
Fountainbridge............................. AZ
Frederick St.................................. AY
Gardner's Crescent...................... AZ 26
George IV Bridge .... BZ 28
George St...................................... ABY
Gloucester Lane .... AY
Grassmarket .... BZ

Hanover St .... BY
Heriot Pl....................................... BZ 29
Heriot Row................................... AY
High Riggs .... AZ
High St.. BY
Holyrood St .... BY
Home St .... AZ
Hope St... AY 31
Howe St.. AY
Jeffrey St....................................... BY
Johnson Terrace........................... ABZ 32
King's Stables Rd .... AYZ
Lady Lawson St .... AZ 33
Lauriston Pl................................... ABZ
Lauriston St.................................. AZ 35
Lawnmarket.................................. BY 36
Leith St.. BY
Leonard's St .... BZ
Leven St .... AZ
Lothian Rd .... AZ
Lothian St...................................... BZ 38
Market St...................................... BY
Meadow Walk .... BZ
Melville Drive............................... AZ
Middle Meadow Walk .... BZ 39
Moray Pl....................................... AY
Morrison St................................... AZ
Mound... BY
Mylne's Court .... BY 40
Nicolson St................................... BZ
North Bridge................................ BY
Parliament Square .... BY 42
Picardy Pl...................................... BY
Pleasance St .... BZ
Ponton St .... AZ 43
Potterrow..................................... BZ
Princes St...................................... ABY
Queen St....................................... ABY

Queensferry	AY	45	South Bridge	BZ	
Regent Rd	BY		Spittal St	AZ	53
Regent Terrace	BY	46	Teviot Pl.	BZ	54
Riddle's Court	BYZ	47	Thornybank	AZ	56
Royal Circus	AY		Victoria St	BZ	57
Royal Terrace	BY		Waterloo Pl.	BY	
St Andrew St	BY	49	Waverly Bridge	BY	59
St David St	BY		Wemyss Pl.	AY	60
St James Centre	BY		West Nicolson St	BZ	61
St Mary's St	BY		West Port	AZ	
St Patrick Square	BZ	50	West Register St	BY	63
Semple St	AZ		West Richmond St	BZ	64
Shandwick Pl.	AY	52	York Pl.	BY	

Edinburgh Festival Fringe

New era of Scottish democracy

The decline of Scottish industry in the 1930s led to frostier relations between Scotland and the central Government, although the Scots had their own legal and education systems. The economic decline of the last decades and discontent about the lack of adequate benefits from North Sea Oil fostered nationalist feelings. The remoteness of central government, the imposition of the poll tax and local government reorganisation were all contentious issues. As direct election of representatives to the European Parliament had given Scotland renewed confidence in its ability to control its own affairs, the 1997 referendum was a resounding vote for devolution.

Scotland greeted the opening of the Scottish Parliament with pride some 290 years after the last parliament was dissolved. The new body opened in Edinburgh on 1 July 1999 and has 120 members; the Executive consists of a First Minister and a team of ministers and law officers. The Parliament has responsibility over wide areas of Scottish affairs and has tax-raising powers. Among areas which remain under Westminster control are the constitution, foreign policy, defence and national security, border controls, economic policy, social security, transport safety and employment legislation.

The parliament's temporary home is the Assembly Hall, off the Royal Mile, but the impressive new 21C buildings at Holyrood eagerly await their new Millennium Scottish Parliamentary representatives.

ce's court at the palace. Many in Edinburgh were like the poet Allan Ramsay who by his departure from the city showed his preference for the peaceful option.

The Enlightenment
In late-18C Edinburgh a circle of great men flourished: Lords of Session Lord Kames, Lord Monbuddo and Lord Hailes, Hugh Blair, historian William Robertson, philosophers David Hume and Dugald Stewart, economist Adam Smith, geologist James Hutton, chemist Joseph Black and architect Robert Adam. Clubs and societies prospered and it was in such a climate of intellectual ferment that plans were put forward for a civic project of great boldness and imagination.

Georgian Edinburgh

Old Edinburgh, on its ridge, was squalid and overcrowded. The earliest moves out were made to George Square in the south before plans for the New Town were drawn up, approved, enacted and accepted socially. The project was encouraged by the early establishment of public buildings in the new area; Theatre Royal (1767-68), Register House (1774-1822), Physicians Hall (1775-77) and the Assembly Rooms (1784-87). Attractive as the elegant streets and squares were, it was to the markets, wynds and closes, taverns and clubs of the Old Town that many still went to earn their livelihood and spend their moments of leisure.

Spanning the two phases of the Enlightenment was Henry Mackenzie, author of *A Man of Feeling*. The second period was dominated by the figures of Scott, Lord Cockburn and Francis Jeffrey. This was the age of the literary magazines, both Whig and Tory (*Edinburgh Review* and *Blackwood's Magazine*); their contributors (Francis Jeffrey, Lockhart, Christopher North, James Hogg and the young Thomas Carlyle) and the publishers and booksellers (Constable, Chambers, Creech). Raeburn, the portraitist, and architects such as Robert Reid, Thomas Hamilton, William Playfair and Gillespie Graham contributed to the making of Athenian Edinburgh.

The interwar years

The 1920-30s period was one of a Scots literary renaissance centred on such literary figures as Hugh MacDiarmid (*Carotid Cornucopions*), Lewis Spence, Neil Gunn, Edwin Muir, Helen Cruickshank, and such haunts as the Abbotsford (Rose St) and the Café Royal. This cultural stirring was reinforced by the launch of the Festival in 1947.

■ People and Culture

One of the first things that a keen-eared visitor to Edinburgh will notice is the number of English and foreign accents in the city, and not just from fellow tourists. Many an English 'migrant' who now works in Edinburgh will tell you that the quality of life is so much higher here than in London or other parts of England.

Edinburgh has always been a cosmopolitan city; its great university and medical establishments attract students from all over the world, while in recent years the global nature of the International and Fringe Festivals has attracted many more overseas visitors and residents. The city may have a reputation for being Anglophile, or at the very least for being less aggressively patriotic than some other Scottish cities – Glasgow, for example – but that doesn't mean its inhabitants are any less committed to the 'Blue Blanket' (the flag of St Andrew).

Edinburgh International Festival

See map of Principal Venues

This prestigious annual festival *(3-week event in August)* provides a quality programme of performances in all art forms. Since its inception in 1947, highlights of the Festival's history have included such specially commissioned works as TS Eliot's *The Cocktail Party* (1948), Peter Maxwell Davies's opera *The Lighthouse* (1980) and the world premiere of *Mörder, Hoffnung der Frauen* by the Ballet Rambert (1983). The ever-popular **Military Tattoo** provides a spectacle rich in colour, tradition, music and excitement under the floodlights of the Castle Esplanade. The capacity audience of 9 000 is entertained by a cast of approximately 600. Also part of Festival time is **The Fringe** with over 700 productions covering a wide range of entertainment. Often avant-garde or just plain eccentric, The Fringe spills out onto the streets and squares of Edinburgh which become the stage for a variety of entertainers from buskers and jugglers to musicians and mime artists.

The sister Edinburgh **Folk Festival,** another annual event, dates from 1979. The entertainments include concerts, lectures and workshops. The **Jazz** and **Film Festivals** which also take place in August are also very popular events.

When visiting Edinburgh during the Festival it is advisable to reserve accommodation in advance. Many museums, galleries and houses extend their opening hours and organise special exhibitions during Festival time

Life in Edinburgh, as in every other modern European city, is imperfect. Begging, usually of the peaceful and passive kind, is prevalent on the streets and at pub closing time it is best to avoid places like the Grassmarket, where groups of booze-fuelled youths (not necessarily from Edinburgh, it must be said) can be unpleasant. On the whole, however, Edinburgh city centre is peaceful and safe, night and day.

Painting

Scottish painting is closely linked with the English artistic tradition as many artists worked in London. Some were also great travellers and were influenced by the evolution of artistic movements in Europe. Many artists, however, remained relatively unknown outside Scotland. There are good holdings of Scottish paintings in the National Galleries in Edinburgh.

The 18C is marked by the portraitist Allan **Ramsay** (1713-84) who was the leader of a group responsible for the founding of Edinburgh's first important art academy and was appointed painter to George III. His delicate portraits of women (*Lady Ann Campbell, Miss Tracy Travell*) are notable. Henry **Raeburn** (1756-1823), George IV's Limner for Scotland, also has a well deserved reputation as a portrait painter (*The Reverend Robert Walker skating, Sir Walter Scott, Mrs Lumsden, Mrs Liddell*). These two artists painted the gentry and leading personalities of the period.

Alexander **Nasmyth** (1785-1859), Ramsay's assistant, became a successful landscape artist (*Robert Burns, The Windings of the Forth, Distant Views of Stirling*). The idealised treatment of nature is illustrated in *The Falls of Clyde* by the neo-Classical master Jacob More. Gavin **Hamilton** (1723-98) painted vast historical compositions (illustrations of Homer's *Illiad, The Abdication of Mary, Queen of Scots*) and became very successful in Rome. In the 19C Walter Scott's novels brought about renewed interest in Scottish landscape: *Glencoe, Loch Katrine, Inverlochy Castle* by Horatio **McCullough** (1805-67) who is famous for his Highland scenes. David **Wilkie's** (1785-1841) artistry is evident in his realistic popular scenes (*Pit-*

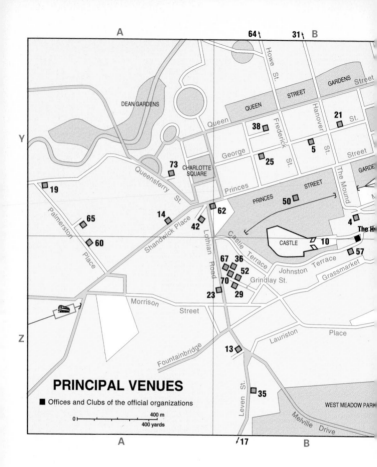

PRINCIPAL VENUES

■ Offices and Clubs of the official organizations

0 |——————| 400 m
0 |——————| 400 yards

lessie Fair, Distraining for Rent) and portraits *(George IV)* which show Raeburn's influence. *The Gentle Shepherd* illustrates Ramsay's pastoral poem.

The Faed brothers (late 19C – early 20C), who were members of an artists' colony in Galloway, specialised in detailed genre scenes. The romantic landscapes and religious works of William **Dyce** (1806-64) heralded the Pre-Raphaelites who influenced Noel Paton (1821-1901). Nature is depicted in great detail in the latter's fairy scenes *(Oberon and Titania)* and other paintings full of symbolism. The portraitist John "Spanish" Phillip (1817-67) is better known for his exotic paintings.

In the Victorian era Highland scenery gained great popularity through the English artist Edwin **Landseer** (1802-73), the official Animal Painter for Scotland, who is famous for his romantic depic-

18

Adam Theatre	CZ	2
Assembly Hall	BY	4
Assembly Rooms	BY	5
Calton Community Centre	CY	8
Calton Studios	CY	9
Castle Esplanade	BZ	10
Central Hall	BZ	13
Cephas Cellar	AY	14
Chaplaincy Centre	CZ	16
Church Hill Theatre	BZ	17
Dance Directions at Belford	AY	19
Festival Club	CZ	
Festival Headquarters	BY	21
Festival Theatre	CZ	22
Filmhouse	ABZ	23
Freemason's Hall	BY	25
Fringe Club	CZ	
Fringe Office	CY	
George Square Theatre	CZ	27
Heriott Watt Theatres	BZ	29
Inverleith House	BY	31
Jazz Festival Office	CY	
Jazz Pavillon	CY	33
King's Theatre	BZ	35
Lyceum Studio	BZ	36
Masonic Lodge	BY	38
Military Tattoo Office	CY	
Netherbow Arts Centre	CY	40
Platform One	AY	42
Playhouse Theatre	CY	43
Pleasance Theatre	CZ	45
Queen's Hall	CZ	47
Reid Concert Hall	CZ	49
Ross Bandstand	BY	50
Royal Lyceum	BZ	52
St Cecilia's Hall	CY	55
St Columba's by the Castle	BZ	57
St Giles Cathedral	CY	58
St Mary's Cathedral	AZ	60
The Hub	BYZ	
Theatre West End	ABY	62
Theatre Workshop	BY	64
Tic-Toc Theatre	AY	65
Traverse Theatre	BZ	67
Usher Hall	BZ	70
Y.W.C.A.	AY	73

tion of Scotland (stags at bay and other Highland scenes). Another Englishman John Everett **Millais** (1829-96), whose wife came from Perthshire and who spent many years near Perth, painted large romantic landscapes *(Chill October)*. The founding of the Scottish Academy in 1836 brought about a flowering of native talent. In reaction against Victorian conventions, William **McTaggart** (1835-1910) developed a highly individual style

– bold brushwork, light effects, rich colours – evident in his dramatic seascapes (*The Storm, Dawn at Sea, The Fishers' Landing*) and landscapes (*Corn in the Ear, Spring, Rosslyn Castle: Autumn*).

Edinburgh's men of letters

Edinburgh has long held a great reputation as an erudite city and has produced two great writers: Sir Walter Scott and Robert Louis Stevenson. **Robert Louis Stevenson** was born in 1850 at 8 Howard Place, North Edinburgh, moving at the age of seven to 17 Heriot Row in the New Town, the house which he immortalised in *The Lamplighter*, a poem from his charming classic collection, *A Child's Garden of Verses* (1885). His first Edinburgh-based book was *Edinburgh, Picturesque No-* tes, which is still very readable today. In 1880 he co-wrote *Deacon Brodie*, perhaps as a prelude to his 1886 classic *The Strange Case of Dr Jekyll and Mr Hyde*. Stevenson was an inveterate traveller throughout his life, spending much time abroad on account of his poor health. In 1883 came his first novel and most popular work, *Treasure Island*; in 1886 *Kidnapped* was published. The following year Stevenson left Edinburgh for the last time, emigrating to America. Ever the adventurer, he sailed the South Seas and bought a house on Samoa, where he settled with his family. He championed the local cause against force colonialism, was treated with great honour and became known as Tusitala ('Teller of Tales'). He stayed in Samoa until he died suddenly in 1894 from a cerebral haemorrhage.

Sir Walter Scott was born in 1771 in College Wynd (now demolished), off Cowgate. The family moved to 25 George Square, where Scott lived until 1797 when he married. He was called to the Scottish Bar in 1792 but his love of romantic literature led in 1802-3 to his first publication, a collection of ballads entitled *The Minstrelsy of the Scottish Border*, which achieved great success. In 1804 he left Edinburgh for country life in Ettrick Forest. After more poems and more success, in 1812 he moved again to his beloved Abbotsford, in the Borders, and began his romantic 'Waverley' novels including *Waverley*, *Guy Mannering*, *Rob Roy* and *The Heart of Midlothian*. Their phenomenal success brought Scott a huge income. Now an international name, this fierce patriot gained even greater fame by petitioning successfully for 'The Honours of Scotland' to be found in Edinburgh Castle. Created a baronet, he organised the historic visit of King George IV to Scotland in 1822 and, with his lavish overuse of archaic Highland Celtic imagery, especially tartan, he set the phoney romantic style for which Scotland is still known today (and for which also, in many quarters, for which Scott is reviled). By 1825, however, the printers and publishers, Ballantynes, in which Scott was a partner, had incurred massive debts. To repay his liabilities, he began five years of incessant writing, during which time his health deteriorated disastrously. Sir Walter Scott died at Abbotsford in 1832 and was buried nearby in Dryburgh Abbey.

Malt whisky

The original spirit was a malt or straight unblended product of a single malt whisky. The quality and subtle differences in character depends essentially on a combination of certain factors: barley not always home grown, water filtered through peat or over granite, equipment such as the shape of the still and the experience and skill of the stillmen. The 116 single malts are classified into Highland, Lowland or Islay.

Blended whisky

Grain whisky is made from malted barley and other cereals. The blends are a mixture of a lighter grain with a malt in secret proportions. Blended varieties are subdivided into two categories: de luxe and standard.

■ Scottish Specialities

Scottish cooking is characterised by the excellence and quality of the natural products from river, moor, sea and farm.

Soups

These number **Cock-a-Leekie** using fowl, cut leeks and prunes; **Scots** or **Barley Broth**, a vegetable and barley soup; **Game Soup; Partan Bree** a crab soup and **Cullen Skink** made with smoked haddock.

Fish

Of the many varieties of fish, pride of place goes to the **salmon**, be it farmed or wild, from the famous fisheries of the Tay, Spey or Tweed. Served fresh or smoked, it is a luxury dish. **Trout** and **salmon-trout** with their delicately pink flesh are equally appreciated. Breakfast menus often feature the **Arbroath Smokie** – a small salted and smoked haddock; the **Finnan Haddie**, a salted haddock dried on the beach prior to smoking over a peat fire; and the **kipper** a split, salted and smoked herring.

Meat

With such first class beef cattle as the Aberdeen Angus and Galloway and home-bred sheep, it is hardly surprising that the quality of Scotch **beef** and **mutton** is unsurpassed. **Haggis** is the national dish.

Desserts

Succulent **soft fruits** (strawberries, raspberries and blackcurrants) ripened slowly in mild sunshine make an excellent sweet. Other creamsweets like **Cranachan** often incorporate one of the soft fruits. **Atholl Brose** is a secret mixture of honey, oatmeal, malt whisky and cream.

Preserves

Heather honey or Scottish-made jam and marmalade make ideal presents.

Whisky, The Water of Life

Today the word whisky conjures up a seemingly endless variety on the shelves of supermarkets (whisky, whiskey, bourbon...) while Scotch Whisky is synonymous with a quality product, which possesses an unrivalled international reputation. The highly competitive whisky industry is Scotland's biggest export earner (over £900 million a year) and one of the government's main sources of revenue (foreign earnings and excise taxes and duty). ■

MAIN SIGHTS

EDINBURGH CASTLE★★★

See city plan and plan of castle

The castle, perched on its strategic **site★★★** on Castle Rock, is impressive from all sides. The silhouette of the castle figures prominently on the skyline of most views of the city, and the castle's role has been of paramount importance throughout the city's history.

Royal residence to military fortress – As early as the 11C the buildings atop Castle Rock were favoured as a residence by royalty, in particular by Margaret, the queen of Malcolm III, and her sons. She in fact died here in 1093 shortly after hearing of the loss of both her liege lord and eldest son at Alnwick.

The castle subsequently alternated between Scottish and English forces and in 1313 suffered demolition by the Scots. In the late 14C Bruce's son, David II, built a tower, of which there are no visible remains, on the site of the Half Moon Battery. The infamous **Black Dinner** of 1440 resulted in the execution of the two young Douglas brothers in the presence of their 10-year-old sovereign, James II, in an attempt to quell Douglas power. James II was born, crowned, married and buried in Edinburgh but it was his son James III who formally recognised the city as his capital.

In the 16C Regent Morton did much to strengthen the castle's defences which suffered again during Sir William Kirkcaldy of Grange's stout defence (1573) in the name of Mary, Queen of Scots. The end result was prompt execution for Grange and repairs and rebuilding to the castle. In the 1650s Cromwell's troops took over and thus began the castle's new role as a garrison. The 18C saw two Jacobite attacks, the last by Bonnie Prince Charlie in person from his headquarters at the other end of the Royal Mile. The buildings we see today are basically those which have resulted from the castle's role as a military garrison in recent centuries.

Esplanade – Created as a spacious parade ground in the 18C, the esplanade is the setting for the Festival's most popular event, the **Military Tattoo** (*see Introduction*), when the floodlit castle acts as backdrop. Before entering, note two of the castle's most imposing features from among the tiers of buildings, the appropriately named Half Moon Battery and the Palace Block towering up behind to the left.

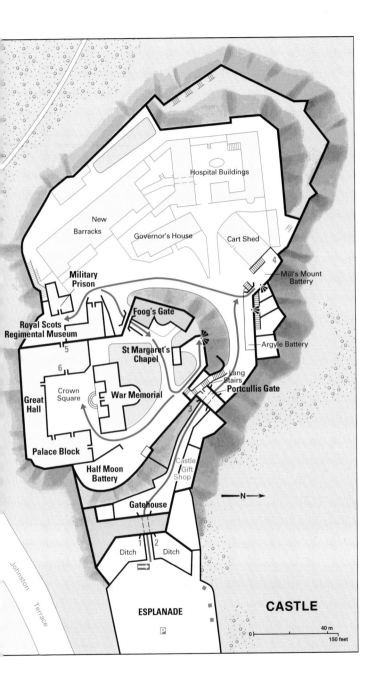

Hospital Buildings

New Barracks

Governor's House

Cart Shed

Mill's Mount Battery

4

Military Prison

Foog's Gate

Royal Scots Regimental Museum

5

6

St Margaret's Chapel

Argyle Battery

Crown Square

War Memorial

Lang Stairs

Portcullis Gate

Great Hall

3

Palace Block

Half Moon Battery

Castle Gift Shop

—N→

Gatehouse

Ditch 1 2 Ditch

ESPLANADE

CASTLE

Johnston Terrace

P

40 m

0

150 feet

27

Gatehouse – Beyond the ditch, started in the 1650s by Cromwell's troops, is the gatehouse, built as a suitably imposing entrance in the 19C. Two national heroes, Bruce (1) and Wallace (2) flank the entrance. Once through, the massive walls of the Half Moon Battery loom up ahead. These demarcate the line of the original outer defences. A plaque (3) on the left, commemorates Kirkcaldy of Grange's stoic defence of 1573.

Portcullis Gate – The lower part, dating from Regent Morton's 1570s fortifications, has decorative features including Morton's coat of arms, while the upper part is a 19C addition.

Further up, the two batteries, Argyle and Mill's Mount, both afford excellent **views**** of Princes Street and the New Town. The daily **one o'clock salute (4)** is fired from the upper battery.

Following the signs round to the left, on the right is the Governor's

View from
North Bridge

House (1742), with adjoining wings for the Master Gunner and Store-Keeper. The imposing building behind is the 1790s New Barracks for the castle garrison.

Royal Scots Regimental Museum – The Royal Regiment is the oldest and most senior regiment of the British Army. Raised on 28 March 1633, the unit originally served under King Louis XIII of France where it earned the nickname of "Pontius Pilate's Bodyguard". The regiment was finally recalled to Britain in 1676; two rooms of exhibits trace the regiment's subsequent history: Corunna, Waterloo, Alma, Sebastopol, Marne... There is an impressive display of medals.

Military Prison – These cells were built in the 1840s.

Vaults (5) – Two levels of great vaulted chambers, situated un-

The Stone of Destiny

According to legend, the stone was Jacob's pillow which eventually reached Ireland by way of Egypt and Spain and is believed to have served as a coronation stone for the High Kings at Tara. The stone was taken to Iona in the 6C where it was presented to St Columba. It was later moved to Dunadd, Dunstaffnage and Dunkeld. After the merger of the kingdoms of the Picts and Scots who originally came from Ireland, Kenneth MacAlpine was the first king to be crowned on the stone at Scone. Subsequently it served for the coronation of all Scottish kings until 1296 when the Scots were defeated by Edward I. He carried off the stone which was placed beneath the Coronation chair in Westminster Abbey where for 700 years it played an integral part of the Coronation rituals. It was stolen in 1950 but was later recovered in Arbroath Abbey.

From early days controversy has raged about the authenticity of the stone. Some believe the original stone never left Scotland. Historians have examined the seals of various kings which show a larger stone while early descriptions mention a large block of black marble with a hollowed-out seat.

In 1996 the people of Scotland greeted the return of the Stone of Destiny, which is the symbol of Scottish nationhood, with great emotion. It is now on display with the Honours of Scotland in Edinburgh Castle and will be returned to Westminster Abbey for future coronations.

der the Crown Square buildings, housed French and American prisoners in the 18C and 19C. In the end chamber stands the 500-year-old siege cannon, **Mons Meg**, resplendent in a new coat of paint. Commissioned by the Duke of Burgundy and forged in 1449 at Mons in Hainaut, it was given eight years later to his nephew James II *(see Index)* who lost his life owing to his enthusiasm for guns. During an eventful career, Mons Meg is said to have served at Crookston (1489), Dumbarton (1489) and

S. Chmith/©ACSI

Norham castles (1497) and even to have spent time in the Tower of London. Sir Walter Scott petitioned for its return and in 1829 the huge medieval cannon was returned to Edinburgh.

Foog's Gate – The original entrance to the upper area of the castle was by stairs (now the Lang Stairs) climbing from beside the Portcullis Gate. With the levelling off of the rest of the Rock, this new entrance was built on the west side.

St Margaret's Chapel – The small rectangular building on the left incorporates remnants of the castle's oldest structure, and perhaps even Edinburgh's. This 12C chapel is dedicated to Malcolm III's Queen Margaret *(see Index)*. Once surrounded by other buildings it served various purposes until the mid 19C when its original role was revealed and restoration ensued. Inside, the chancel arch is Norman in inspiration with its cushion capitals and chevron decoration.

The terrace in front offers an extensive **panorama***** of northern Edinburgh, in particular Princes Street and the gardens, and the geometric pattern of the New Town.

Half Moon Battery – The battery was built following the 1573 siege, which saw the destruction of David II's tower house. From here the strategic importance of the original tower with its command of castle approaches and entrance is evident.

The heart of the medieval fortress and one-time royal residence is marked by Crown Square. Of the four buildings overlooking the square today only the southern and eastern ranges are of historic interest.

Scottish National War Memorial – *North side*. In the 1920s **Robert Lorimer** *(see Index)* undertook the task of converting a mid-18C building into Scotland's War Memorial. The exterior, with a strong resemblance to the palace part of Stirling Castle, is in harmony with the earlier buildings.

The interior achieves a suitable atmosphere of dignity and reverence to honour those who served. Wartime scenes are the subject of the attractive stained-glass round-headed windows by Douglas Strachan. The low-relief sculptures depict the fighting men and other participants in the struggle. A casket containing the names of the fallen stands in the apse.

Scottish United Services Museum (6) – *West side. East gallery in Palace Block*. This section of the museum houses displays of uniforms, medals, badges, Colours and weapons illustrating the history of the Scottish regiments of the British Army.

Great Hall – *South side*. The hall built in the late 15C for James IV succeeded a series of earlier buildings. The chief attraction of this spacious apartment intended for great occasions is the **hammer-beam roof★★** which can be fully appreciated since the 19C restoration. Boards and beams are attractively painted and reward inspection.

Palace Block – *East side*. This range, which dates from the 15C, contained the royal apartments overlooking the old town. The interior was remodelled for James VI's only return visit to Scotland in 1617.

Enter by the door nearest the Great Hall range. A room on the right has displays on excavations at Mill's Mount dating back to the Iron Age. Straight ahead, Queen Mary's Room is hung with family portraits of her son James VI, her grandson Charles I, her great-grandsons Charles II and James II and her first husband Francis II. There is also a plaster cast from Mary's tomb effigy at Westminster Abbey. The adjoining small **chamber**, with its panelling and timber ceiling, is the room where James VI was born in 1566. The decoration dates from the 1617 refurbishing. Once in the square again, the doorway in the staircase tower leads to the Crown Chamber on the first floor where the **Honours of Scotland★★★** are displayed. Fol-

lowing the Union of Parliaments in 1707, they were sealed up in this chamber and it was on Sir Walter Scott's initiative that they were rediscovered. Although of unknown age, the pearl and gem encrusted **crown** is Britain's only pre-Restoration crown to have escaped being melted down by Cromwell. The **sceptre** and **sword** were gifts from two Popes to the Renaissance prince, James IV, the former from the Borgia Pope, Alexander VI (1492-1503), and the latter from his successor, Pope Julius II (1503-13), a great patron of the arts. Pride of place is also given to the **Stone of Destiny**, the ancient symbol of Celtic kingship, which was returned to Scotland in 1996 after 700 years under the Coronation Chair at Westminster Abbey.

The other rooms (East Gallery) contain further displays on the Royal Navy, Royal Air Force, Scotland's sole cavalry regiment, the Royal Scots Greys (see Index), and the yeomanry regiments. Note the model of the pride of James IV's navy, the magnificent **Great Michael** (1507-11). Rival to Henry's Great Harry (1512), like most of the Scottish fleet she set sail in 1513 to support the French King facing the threat of the Holy League. She was eventually sold to Louis XII. ∎

View down to Princes street from the castle

HOLYROODHOUSE

At the east end of the Royal Mile stands the Palace of Holyroodhouse, the Queen's official residence in Scotland, adjoined by the ruined nave of the abbey. In the background are the green slopes and rocky crags of Holyrood Park rising to Arthur's Seat.

The Holy Rood – Legend has it that **David I**, while out hunting, was thrown from his mount and wounded by a stag. In a defensive gesture he made to grasp the animal's antlers only to find he was holding a crucifix, the animal having made off into the forest. In recognition David founded the Augustinian Abbey of Holy Rood in 1128 and granted to the canons the right to their own burgh, Canongate.

The medieval abbey prospered and benefited from royal patronage in the 15C from the Stewart Kings. James II was born, married and buried here and broke with the Scone tradition to be crowned here. His three successors were all married in the abbey. It was during this period that the guesthouse was used as a royal residence in preference to the castle. James IV, intent on making Edinburgh his capital, started transforming the guest house accommodation into a palace by building the present northwest tower.

Work continued after his death at Flodden (1513). The abbey buildings suffered damage in 1544, were despoiled at the Reformation and burnt in 1650 when Cromwell's troops were quartered there. A moment of glory in the interval was the coronation of Charles I in 1633. From then on the nave served as parish church for the Canongate until 1688, when the congregation was dislodged by James VII who intended converting it into a Chapel Royal and the headquarters of the Order of the Thistle.

H. Wood, D. Corrance & M. Alexander and ELFB

Palace of Holyroodhouse

Royal palace – Although Charles II never set foot in the palace he commissioned **Sir William Bruce** (1630-1710), the Architect Royal, to draw up designs. The architect had been instrumental – acting as an envoy – in Charles II's restoration. Bruce may have been influenced by designs for Whitehall done by Inigo Jones, as the final result is a handsome example of the Palladian style.

Bruce and his master mason, **Robert Mylne** (1633-1710), created a masterpiece of elegance, particularly in the courtyard elevations. They cleverly retained the 16C northwest tower counterbalancing it with a second.

Royal residents – Following Mary, Queen of Scots' six-year stay, the next royal occupant was James, Duke of York (future James VII) from 1679 to 1682 in his capacity as Commissioner for his brother Charles II. With Bonnie Prince Charlie, there was a brief period of royal receptions when he made Holyroodhouse his headquarters prior to his ultimate defeat at Culloden (see Index). George IV held a levee in 1822 and there were two periods of occupation by a French royal, firstly as Comte d'Artois having fled the Revolution and secondly as the exiled Charles X after his abdication in 1830. Since the reign of Queen Victoria, the palace has again been favoured as a royal residence.

■ **Palace** *1hr*

Exterior – The fountain is a 19C copy of the one at Linlithgow. The entrance front was the last part of the palace to be rebuilt as it had originally been intended to retain the front built by James IV.

Counterbalancing the towers is the elaborate entrance. Flanked by columns, the door is surmounted by carved stonework incorporating the Scottish coat of arms (note the unicorn supporters), a broken pediment, a cupola and crown. The inner court elevations are an outstanding example of classic Renaissance of the Stuart Period and one of Scotland's earliest examples. The superimposed orders, general proportions, arcades and pediment are applied in the purest Classical manner achieving a composition of restraint, symmetry and elegance.

Interior – The decoration of the State Apartments remains lavish as designed by Sir William Bruce in true Restoration style. Highly intricate decorative plasterwork ceilings, lavishly carved woodwork (doors, doorcases, picture frames and swags) and inset canvases were all integral parts of the decor and all of a very high standard of craftsmanship. The seven outstanding **plasterwork ceilings***** in high relief represent 10 years' labour by the "gentlemen modellers" **John Halbert** and **George Dunsterfield.** These craftsmen had previously worked at Ham House, the London home of the Lauderdales *(see Index),* patrons and relatives of Bruce, and at Windsor for Charles II.

The impressive Grand Staircase leads up past Her Majesty's portrait by Her Limner, David Donald-son. Other than the ceilings, the most notable features of the **State Apartments** are: in the Adam-style Dining-Room a splendid portrait of *George IV in Highland Dress* by Sir David Wilkie. In the Throne Room, redecorated in the 1920s, are royal portraits of the brothers Charles II and James VII (the palace's first royal guest) with their respective queens, and Queen Victoria in her coronation robes. Carved door surrounds and 18C Brussels tapestries (market scenes, Asia, Africa) can be seen in the Evening Drawing Room. Finest of all is the Morning Drawing-Room sumptuously decorated with a Jacob de Wet medallion above the fireplace and 17C French tapestries (the Story of Diana). The King's Suite was on the east side, overlooking the famous Privy Garden of formal design on the site of the demolished cloister.

In the King's Chamber is a magnificent Red Bed (1672) and ceiling with a De Wet medallion depicting the Apotheosis of Hercules, which is similar to the one in the Vine Room at Kellie Castle. Note the pairs of animals looking down. The Gallery walls are lined with many imaginary and a few real portraits of Scottish Kings from 6C Fergus to James VII. Jacob de Wet completed the portraits in two years.

The **Historic Apartments** in the 16C round tower consist of similar suites on two floors. These were refurbished c 1672 when floor and ceiling levels were adjusted to correspond to the Bruce additions. There are many Mary, Queen of Scots associations. The antechamber has 17C Mortlake tapestries from the workshop founded by her son James VI. Upstairs are two exquisite **16C coffered ceilings**, the first adorned with painted designs. The small chamber adjoining the Bedchamber is closely associated with the murder of Mary's Italian secretary, Rizzio, in 1566. His body was found in the outer chamber (brass plaque marks the spot). Paintings depict Mary's 2nd husband, **Henry Lord Darnley** (1546-67), as a 17-year-old youth with his brother. A second work shows his mourning family, including his son James VI, after Darnley's murder at Kirk o'Field (see Index). On the way downstairs note Medina's portrait of the palace architect, Sir William Bruce.

■ Abbey *15min*

The roofless nave is all that remains of this once great abbey. It dates mainly from the late 12C and early 13C and there are some finely sculpted details. Compare the interlaced round-headed blind arcading of the 12C in the north aisle with the pointed 13C work opposite. The south elevation is an attractive fragment of 13C design. Queen Victoria rebuilt the royal burial vault following its destruction on the departure of the Roman Catholic James VII. The remains of David II, James II, James V and Lord Darnley are interred here. Of the west front, the remaining flanking tower, recessed pointed doorway and different levels of arcading give some impression of what the whole must have looked like. Note the medallion portraits.

■ Holyrood Park

Holyrood Park, the largest area of open ground within the city, is dominated by Arthur's Seat (823ft/251m) and the Salisbury Crags, both volcanic features. A path from the car park on the Queen's Road, within the park, leads up to **Arthur's Seat** *(30min)* which affords a tremendous **panorama**★★ of the Edinburgh area.

At the foot of Arthur's Seat, the historic palace buildings are offset by significant structures reflecting the town's dynamic outlook following the devolution of power to Scotland: the futuristic Dynamic Earth *(see Index)*; the spectacular Scottish Parliament building *(under construction)*; another new building accommodating the offices of the Scotsman.

Beyond Dunsapie lies the village of **Duddingston** in an attractive setting between park and loch (bird sanctuary). The 12C church has some good Norman features. ■

ROYAL MILE**

The principal thoroughfare of the Old Town runs from the castle, in its strategic site, down the ridge to the abbey and palace. The Royal Mile is in fact a succession of four streets: Castle Hill, the Lawnmarket, the High Street and the Canongate. Daniel Defoe wrote in the early 18C, "This is, perhaps, the largest, longest, and finest street for buildings and number of inhabitants, not in Britain only, but in the world". The few original buildings which remain give some idea of what medieval Edinburgh must have looked like. Plaques on the pends record the famous and infamous occupants and historic events associated with the closes.

Ramsay Gardens on the left incorporate **Ramsay Lodge** built in the 18C by the poet Allan Ramsay (1686-1758), father of the portrait painter of the same name.

The Scotch Whisky Heritage Centre – The ground floor exhibition traces the whisky-making process from peat making to bottling and packaging. A 10min film "The Water of Life" explains the different types of whisky and the workings and layout of a

H. Wood, D. Corrance & M. Alexander and ELTB

typical Speyside distillery. Upstairs, a ride through a series of lifelike tableaux gives a pictorial account of whisky making.

Outlook Tower and Camera Obscura – From its rooftop position in the Outlook Tower, the **camera obscura** presents a fascinating view of the city. Exhibitions deal with holography, pin-hole photography and space photography.

The Church of Scotland **General Assembly Hall** stands on the site of what was Mary of Guise's Palace (destroyed 1861). The Hall is the temporary home of the Debating Chamber of the Scottish Parliament, pending the completion of the new Parliament Building at Holyrood.

Enter **Mylne's Court**, a 1970s reconstruction, to have some idea of what a court looked like once a narrow burgess strip had been built over. The narrow approach passages from the main street are known as closes or wynds.

The Hub – A tall steeple highlights the former Highland Tolbooth, built in the mid 19C by James Gillespie Graham and Augustus Pugin and now imaginatively refurbished as

Old Town skyline

Edinburgh's Festival Centre. The ornate interior boasts contemporary sculpture, tiling and stained glass as well as a splendid sculpture hall. The Hub will be a focal point for the city's festivals.

Gladstone's Land* – This narrow six-storey land (tenement) is typical of 17C Edinburgh when all building was upwards. The property was acquired in 1617 by a merchant burgess, Thomas Gledstanes, who rebuilt and extended it out towards the street. The premises behind the pavement arcade are arranged as a shop with living quarters on the other floors. The first floor is a good example of a 17C town house: original **painted ceilings** and 17C carved Scottish bed and Dutch chests.

Lady Stair's House – *Down the close*. Built in 1622, this town house takes its name from an occupant of the late 18C, the widow of John Dalrymple, 1st Earl of Stair. It is now home to the **Writers' Museum** which displays manuscripts, relics and other memorabilia of three of Scotland's greatest literary figures: Robert Burns (1759-96), Sir Walter Scott (1771-1832) and R L Stevenson (1850-94).

In **Riddle's Court** go through to the second courtyard which is overlooked on the south side by **Bailie MacMorran's House**. It was here that the burgesses of Edinburgh laid on a banquet in 1598 for James VI and Anne of Denmark.

St Giles' Cathedral** – *See cathedral plan.* The present High Kirk of Edinburgh is probably the third church on this site. The first, dating from the 9C, was probably closer to the castle. It was replaced by a Romanesque structure in 1126 of which remain the four piers supporting the tower. This was burnt down by the English in 1385 following which the present building was raised. Alterations and restorations have radically changed the character of the 15C church. The Reformation brought troubled times to St Giles', when the many altars and images, including the precious relic and statue of St Giles, were swept away, the latter into the Nor'Loch. For a short spell St Giles' alternated between Reformed and Catholic control before the return of **Knox** as minister in 1560. Shortly after began his period of confrontation with Mary, Queen of Scots. As the capital's principal church it served as meeting place for Parliament and the General Assembly and witnessed many great state occasions such as James VI's farewell to his Scottish subjects and, over 200 years later, George IV's 1822 state visit.

The Jenny Geddes stool-throwing incident (a protest against Episcopacy – statue and plaque on the north side of the Moray aisle), although much disputed histori-cally, preceded the signing of the National Covenant (see the Linli-thgow copy in the Chepman aisle) and the ensuing religious strife. Twice during the 17C the church enjoyed a brief spell of cathedral status (1637-38 and 1661-89).

Exterior – Seen from the west, the church is dominated by the square tower raising aloft the delicate **crown spire*** (1495), a most distinctive feature of Edinburgh's skyline. The imperial or eight-ar-ched design differentiates it from that of King's College, Aberdeen. The church's exterior lost much of its original character when it was refaced (19C).

Interior – The original cruciform shape has been lost with the ad-dition of aisle and side chapels. Although the interior was spared the systematic restoration of the exterior, details, and in particular monuments, provide the main points of interest.

Start in the northwest corner and proceed in a clockwise direction.

The flowing style and strong glowing colours of the north aisle window (1) characterise the work of the Pre-Raphaelites, Burne-Jones and William Morris. In the north aisle stands Pittendrigh MacGilli-vray's statue of **John Knox** (1512-72) (2), reformer and minister of St Giles'. The Albany Aisle with its Gothic vaulting was probably built in expiation for the murder of the Duke of Rothesay (see Index) in 1402. The aisle beyond contains the imposing 19C marble monument (3) to the 8th Earl and 1st Marquess of Argyll (1607-61) who was executed at the mercat cross only days after the body of his arch rival the Marquess of Montrose had been rehabilitated and interred on the far side of the church. The heraldic window decorated with coats of arms of leading Covenanters is a reminder of the earl's Covenanting loyalties. Move back into the south transept to admire Douglas Strachan's great north window (4), a glow of blue above the carved stone screen. From here also admire the attrac-tive 15C rib and groin vaulting of the chancel and compare it with that of the nave (19C).

In 1911 Robert Lorimer designed the **Thistle Chapel** in the Flam-boyant Gothic style for the most Noble Order of the Thistle foun-ded by James VII in 1687. Some claim it was a revival of an even older foundation. Under a fan-vaulted ceiling and its multitude of carved bosses, some tinctured and many heraldic, are the richly carved stalls and canopies for the sovereign and 16 knights. It is a lavishly impressive display of 20C craftsmanship. Above are helmets, crests and banners with knights' arms on the stall backs.

← —N—

Thistle Chapel

CHANCEL

Preston aisle

Shop

Royal   Mile   High   Street

Chambers aisle

Chepman aisle

5

4

☐

SANCTUARY

Organ

3   St Eloi's aisle

6   7

Moray aisle

NAVE

8

Albany aisle

2

1

ST GILES

Parliament   Square

0 |——| 5 m
0 |————| 20 feet

Beyond the Preston aisle is the side chapel known as the Chepman aisle, in memory of the man who introduced printing into Scotland in the reign of James IV (1488-1513). The aisle is the final resting place of the **Marquess of Montrose** (1612-50) **(5)**, Covenanter and Royalist whose fame rests on his brilliant 1644-45 campaign. He suffered an ignominious fate at the hands of his enemy, Argyll. The Restoration meant rehabilitation for Montrose and a traitor's execution for Argyll.

The aisle beyond the organ has a 19C marble monument **(6)** to James Stewart, Earl of Moray (1531-70), with an original 16C brass. Half-brother to Mary, Queen of Scots and Regent for her son, Moray was murdered in Linlithgow in 1570. A window **(7)** by Noel Paton relates the tale and shows Knox preaching at the funeral service of one of his strongest supporters.

The low relief **(8)** at the end of the Moray Aisle portrays Robert Louis Stevenson (1850-94), offspring of a family of engineers, who achieved fame as an author.

The imposing buildings at the corner of the Lawnmarket and George IV Bridge are the **Committee Chambers**. They contain the **Scottish Parliament Visitor Centre** which provides information about all aspects of the Scottish Parliament. The Signet Library to the rear of the cathedral dates from 1810-12. Near the Boehm statue of the 5th Duke of Buccleuch in Garter Robes is a heart shape set into the cobbles. This marks the site of the old tolbooth (1466-1817) made famous by Scott in *The Heart of Midlothian*.

Parliament Hall – Behind the imposing Georgian façade is the 17C Parliament Hall decreed by Charles I and designed by his master mason **John Mylne**. Where the Scottish Parliament met from 1639 to 1707, lawyers now pace under the carved and gilded **hammerbeam roof** and the gaze of their august predecessors: Duncan Forbes (Roubiliac); Sir Adam Cockburn (Brodie); Scott; 1st Viscount Melville (Chantrey) and his nephew, Robert Dundas (also Chantrey); Viscount Stair (Aikman), author of *Stairs Institutes* (1681), and his contemporary Sir George Mackenzie, known as "Bluidy Mackenzie" in Covenanting history, but best remembered for his standard work on Scottish law and as founder of the Advocate's Library, today Scotland's National Library; and Lord Monbuddo, an 18C eccentric.

It was Lord Cockburn who said, "The old building exhibited some respectable turrets, some ornamental windows and doors and a handsome balustrade". The great window depicts the inauguration of the College of Justice. In the foreground is the Lord Chancellor Gavin Dunbar with Alexander Mylne, Abbot of Cambuskenneth and the first President, with the Papal Bull before James V and his court. South of St Giles' is an equestrian statue of the Merry Monarch, Charles II (1685), the oldest in Edinburgh.

At the east end is the **mercat cross**, where merchants and traders congregated to transact business and the scene of celebrations, demonstrations, executions and royal proclamations. The 19C structure incorporates the shaft of the 16C cross.

City Chambers – The former Royal Exchange was built in 1753 to replace the mercat cross as a meeting place. The front, facing Cockburn Street, is 11 storeys high. The screen at pavement level shelters the City's Stone of Remembrance.

The first edition of *Encyclopaedia Britannica* was printed between 1768-71 in **Anchor Close**. The original compilers were William Smellie, Colin Macfarquhar and Andrew Bell. They purposely avoided the encyclopaedic dictionary form and their solution became the model for later English language encyclopaedias. The *Encyclopaedia Britannica* still bears a thistle on the covers.

Tron Kirk – John Mylne built this church prior to undertaking Parliament Hall. The spire is a 19C replacement. This is the traditional gathering place of Hogmanay revellers.

Museum of Childhood – Anything and everything to do with childhood is the theme of this unique museum. Displays include toys, costumes, books, dolls and games. Children discover while parents reminisce.

Brass Rubbing Centre – *Chalmers' Close*. Try your hand at brass rubbing and choose from a varied collection of replicas of Pictish stones and brasses.

Further along the street, 15C **Mowbray House** was the studio of the portraitist **George Jamesone** (1588-1644).

John Knox House – This picturesque town house was probably built prior to 1490. The armorial panel on the west wall is that of the goldsmith, James Mossman, whose father was responsible for redesigning the Scottish crown. The **John Knox** connection is now much contested but the house and its exhibits provide an insight into the man, his beliefs and Scotland during the Reformation. The main room on the second floor has a painted ceiling (1600).

The junction with St Mary's and Jeffrey Streets marks the site of the Netherbow Port. The arched gateway with a tower and spire was demolished in 1764.

Beyond was the independent burgh of **Canongate** (gait or way of the canons) where the nobility, ambassadors and other royal officers built residences in close proximity to the royal palace of Holyroodhouse. Only a few of these mansions remain.

The gateway with pyramidal posts and adjoining gable-ended building with first floor balcony are all that remain of **Moray House**, now better known as a College of Education. Tradition has it rightly or wrongly that it was in the summer house of this residence that the Treaty of Union of 1707 was signed.

Canongate Tolbooth* – Tolbooth for the independent burgh of Canongate, this building with its turreted steeple was built in 1591 and is a good example of 16C architecture. The tolbooth houses the People's Story Museum.

People's Story Museum – The museum gives a moving insight into the daily life and work of the citizens from the late 18C to the present day: tableaux, documents, photographs, oral and written testimonies etc.

Canongate Church – This church was built in 1688 for the displaced congregation of Holyrood Abbey when James VII decided to convert the nave into a Chapel Royal for the Most Ancient Order of the Thistle. Above the curvilinear south front is a stag's head bearing a cross, a reminder of the founding legend of Holyrood Abbey. Inside, the royal pew and those of officers of the Royal Household are indicated by coats of arms. Interesting memorials in the churchyard include that of Adam Smith and the young Edinburgh poet Robert Fergusson, whose tombstone was paid for by Burns. Another Burns connection is the plaque to Clarinda (east wall).

Huntly House – These three 16C mansions now contain the main city museum of local history. Some of the rooms (9-11) have 18C Memel panelling. The Edinburgh silver collection (9-10) contains some particularly fine 18C pieces. The museum has an original parchment of the National Covenant.

Dynamic Earth – *Opposite Palace of Holyroodhouse.* Against the stark backdrop of the Salisbury Crags rises a striking building with a tented roof designed by Sir Michael Hopkins (1999). An innovative exhibition using state-of-the-art interpretative technology unravels the story of the planet: the Big Bang, the formation of the solar system, volcanoes and earthquakes, glaciers, the evolution of life, the extinction of animal and plant species, the beauty and power of the oceans. Life in the polar regions is dramatically contrasted with the environment of the tundra and rainforest. A stone amphitheatre which seats 1 000 spectators hosts special events.

Another landmark nearby is the new Scottish Parliament building. The original design by Enric Mirales comprises clusters of small buildings shaped like up-turned boats, connected by glass walkways. ■

Eating out on the Royal Mile

SOUTH OF THE ROYAL MILE

Royal Mile to George Heriot's School
See city plan

Victoria Street* – Descending in a curve to the Grassmarket, this street is lined with an attractive series of boutiques.

Grassmarket – The railed enclosure marks the site of the gallows where Captain Porteous was hanged (1736) and over 100 Covenanters were martyred. At the southwest corner, **West Port** marks the city's western gate. It was from a close nearby that the bodys-

natchers Burke and Hare operated.

Cowgate – Although outside the original town wall, this was a fashionable quarter in the 16C. It is now a forlorn underpass.

Curving upwards, Candlemaker Row leads to George IV Bridge, passing the **statue** of a dog, Greyfriars Bobby *(see below)*, on the left, at the top.

Greyfriars Church and Churchyard – The 1612 church built on the site of a 15C Franciscan friary has been much altered. The church is known in history as the place where the **National Covenant** (1638) was signed (copy inside). The churchyard memorials include the Martyrs Monument (northeast wall) to the Covenanters taken at Bothwell Brig (1679) and imprisoned here for five months, and the grave over which Bobby, the faithful Skye terrier, stood watch for 14 years.

Take Forrest Road to Lauriston Place. During the daytime when the gate is open, the churchyard ex-tension offers a short cut to George Heriot's School.

George Heriot's School – *Walk round the outside and into the courtyard.*

This great Edinburgh school was endowed by **George Heriot** (1563-1624), goldsmith to James VI who nicknamed him "Jinglin Geordie". On his death, Heriot bequeathed the fortune he had made in London to the city fathers, for the education of "fatherless bairns of Edinburgh freemen". Construction was begun by William Wallace in 1628 but completion was delayed until 1659 when the building was used as a hospital by Cromwell's troops. The symmetrical courtyard building is a good example of an early Renaissance edifice with abundant decorative stone carving and strapwork. The clock tower and statue of Geordie overlooking the courtyard are the work of Robert Mylne (1693).

A fragment of the **Flodden Wall** can be seen to the west of the school, at the head of the Vennel. Opposite is the 1879 Royal Infirmary.

To reach George Square take Meadow Walk past Rowand Anderson's Medical School. ■

UNIVERSITY CAMPUS

George Square to Chambers Street
See city plan

George Square – The square, laid out in the 1760s, was the first major residential development outside the Old Town. Distinguished residents included Scott (no 25 west side) and the Duchess of Gordon. The west side is the only complete example of the vernacular Classical style. The remaining sides are occupied by the university: library (1967) by Basil Spence; David Hume Tower (1963) for the Faculty of Social Sciences and the Science Faculty in Appleton Tower (1966).

The Meadows – Beyond the Ancient Royalty, this once fashionable place of promenade was part of the Burgh Muir. Here Scottish armies rallied and the town council held wappenschaws where arms were paraded.

Leave by Charles Street. The round building on the far side of the pedestrian precinct, Bristo Square, is Rowand Anderson's Victorian McEwan Hall. The Student Centre is the home of the Fringe Club during the Festival.

Old University – The Old College was founded in 1581 and occupied premises within Kirk o'Field Collegiate Church (f 1450) *(see Index)* outside the city walls. It was here that Lord Darnley met his death. In 1789 **Robert Adam** provided a grandiose design for a double courtyard building. Only the main front with impressive entrance overlooking South Bridge is his work. Playfair modified the design to one courtyard and completed the surrounding ranges. The **Talbot Rice Gallery** *(enter from southwest corner, first floor)* occupies Playfair's Georgian gallery, the original home of the Industrial Museum. The permanent Torrie Collection alternates with travelling exhibitions.

Chambers Street – Mid-Victorian slum clearance at the instigation of Lord Provost Chambers obliterated Adam, Argyle and Brown squares, when South Bridge and George IV Bridge were linked by this splendid thoroughfare. The north range of Old College and the Royal Museum of Scotland occupy the south side. Opposite is the Adam Theatre, followed by the University Staff Club (nos 9-15) remodelled in the 1950s by Basil Spence. The latter houses the Festival Club. Beyond is the former **Heriot Watt University** (no 23). The original institute was founded in 1821 and renamed as a memorial to James Watt. With the demolition of Adam Square the institute took up premises at

no 23. A second name change followed in 1885 to Heriot Watt College, with a status change to that of university in 1965. The campus is at Riccarton Estate, south of the city limits. The building is now used as Law Courts.

Royal Museum of Scotland*
– *Chambers Street.* One of the legacies of the 1851 Great Exhibition was the proliferation of many museums and art galleries throughout Britain. Funds were allocated to Edinburgh in 1854 for the foundation of the Industrial Museum. Capt Fowke RE of Albert Hall fame designed the building with an elaborate Venetian Renaissance-style façade contrasts. In stimulating contrast to this masterpiece of Victorian cast iron and plate glass construction is the landmark building opened in 1998 to house the collections now grouped under the title of the **Museum of Scotland**. Faced in Clasach sandstone from Morayshire, the exterior of this striking new structure features a **drum tower** overlooking the junction of Chambers Street with George IV Bridge, and, in contrast to traditional museum buildings, has windows offering passers-by glimpses of the riches within. Inside, an almost bewildering variety of internal spaces ranges from the sublimely light and airy **Hawthornden Court** to mysterious cavities set deep below ground. Spiral staircases seem contained within the thickness of massive walls, while balconies, galleries and windows create stimulating visual relationships both within the building and beyond it to the outside world.

The new building has permitted the display of much more of the extraordinarily rich and varied Scottish collections. This, together with imaginative and innovative presentation, make a visit to this part of the museum an essential and enjoyable first step in grasping the essence of the land and its people.

Entered from Chambers Street, the spacious, well-lit **Main Hall** forms the vestibule of the museum, with access both to the older galleries and, via the Hall of Power, to the Hawthornden Court and the displays of the Museum of Scotland.

Museum of Scotland

Access to the Museum of Scotland is also from the tower at the junction of Chambers Street and George IV Bridge. Free orientation tours are available at various times throughout the day and are recommended.

The left hand column identifies themes while the right hand column generally highlights particularly important items.

Level 0 *(basement)*

Beginnings

The building blocks of Scotland	Spectacular rock specimens, including 2 900 million year old Lewisian gneiss
History of the Wildlife	Dioramas of tundra, oakwood and Caledonian pine forest

Early People

(Scotland's inhabitants from c 8000 BC to AD 1100)	Figures by Sir Eduardo Paolozzi
	8C-9C carved stone from Ross and Cromarty with hunting scene
	Sculpted stone from Angus of rider drinking from horn
	6C-8C BC "Goddess" figure from Ballachulish
	Roman funerary sculpture of devouring lioness
	Roman carnyx or war horn
	Silver treasure from Traprain Law, East Lothian

Level 1 *(Street Level, off Hawthornden Court)*

The Kingdom of the Scots

(Scotland from its emergence as a nation to the 1707 Act of Union)

Scotland Defined	9C cross from Dupplin, Perthshire
	Monymusk reliquary made to hold relic of St Columba
	12C Lewis chesspieces
	Early 16C carving of St Andrew
The Gael	Highland brooches
	Clarsach (harp)
Monarchy and Power	The "Maiden" beheading machine
The Renaissance	Painted ceiling from Rossend Castle
Burghs – Life in towns	
The Medieval Church	8C St Fillan crozier
The Reformed Church	
New Horizons – Scotland in the 17C	Portrait of Esther Inglis

Level 3 Scotland Transformed 1707-1914

Living on the Land	*Reconstructed cruck-built Dunbartonshire house*
Power	*Late-18C Newcomen atmospheric engine from Ayrshire coal mine*
Trade and Industry	*Serf's collar*
The Jacobite Challenge	*Bonnie Prince Charlie's silver travelling canteen*
The Spirit of the Age	*Reconstruction of 18C Edinburgh room with painted panels*
The Church	*Communion vessels*
Daith Comes In (Level 4)	*Late-18C hearse decorated with skulls and hourglasses*

Levels 4/5 Industry and Empire

The Workshop of the World (Level 4)	*Distilling, ship models, 1861 locomotive Ellesmere*
Scottish Pottery	
Victorians and Edwardians	*Work by Charles Rennie Mackintosh, Sir Robert Lorimer, Phoebe Traquair and Glasgow women artists*
The Silver Treasury	*Changing displays of Scottish silver from 16C onwards*
Innovators	*18C and 19C scientists, explorers, politicians and artists*
Scotland and the World	*Scots abroad*

Level 6 Twentieth Century

An extraordinary array of objects chosen by children and adults to represent Scotland in the 20C.

The **Roof Terrace** gives a most unusual **panorama** over castle and city.

International Galleries

Ground Floor

Asiatic sculpture, Classical and Middle Eastern art (1,3,4)	*Assyrian king and courtier* *Cedarwood totem pole from British Columbia*
Temporary exhibitions (2)	
Natural Curiosity (6)	
Evolution (7)	*350 million year old fish fossils*
Mammals (8)	*78ft/24m long Blue Whale skeleton*
Carnivores and Reptiles (10)	
World in Our Hands (A/V show) (11)	
British Animals and Birds (12, 13)	
Art and Industry since 1850	*Bauhaus products, bubble car*

First Floor

European Art 1200-2000 (2)	15C Birth of the Virgin from Lübeck, Lennoxlove Toilet Service, Beaton
Panels c 1540.	
Ceramics (3)	Charles II slipware dish
Glass (4)	Luther glass c 1845
Western Decorative Art 1850-2000 (5,6)	Phoebe Traquair enamel c 1890,
German silver nef pre-1874	
Insects and Molluscs (7, 11,12)	Papier-mâché teaching beetle
Enamels and Silver (14)	
Modern Jewellery (17)	Miss Crowford Collection
Costume (18)	
Ancient Egypt (20)	Dioramas of Egyptian life

Second Floor

Ivy Wu Gallery of Far Eastern Art (2)	Hokusai comic strip, Hiroshige 100 Views of Edo, 1719 model of Dutch East Indiaman "D'Bataviase Eeuw"
China (3), Islam and Japan (4)	16C-17C Turkish dish
Minerals and Gems (7)	Scottish agates
Geology (8), Skeletons (9), Fossils (10)	
Rocks and Minerals (11)	
Within the Middle East (12)	Embroidered hanging from Kerman, Iran
Invertebrates (13)	9'6" Giant Japanese Spider-Crab
Arms and Armour (14)	14C Pembridge Helm
Instruments of Science (18)	Napier's "Bones"
Tribal Art (20)	Benin hornblower, New Ireland helmet mask

NEW TOWN**

See city plan

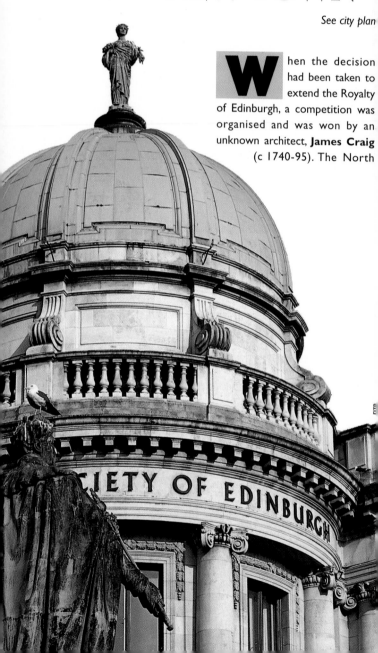

When the decision had been taken to extend the Royalty of Edinburgh, a competition was organised and was won by an unknown architect, **James Craig** (c 1740-95). The North

Bridge was thrown across the valley and the development of Edinburgh's New Town proceeded apace. The project was to be entirely residential at the outset – business and commerce were to remain in the Old Town centred on the Royal Exchange – and the winning plan had a gridiron layout in which vistas and focal points played an important role.

The plan was adhered to, giving a succession of splendid squares and elegant streets. Initially strict architectural uniformity was lacking, although by 1782 a series of regulations had been established concerning the number of storeys, width of façade... The success was immediate and people were quick to follow the example of Hume and Lord Cockburn in taking up residence.

Development continued with a variety of extensions, notably to the north with the Second New Town, northwest with the Moray Estate and also to the west and east. The New Town with its unique quality, its many gardens and green spaces, is one of the finest town planning ventures. The guardian of the 766 acres of the splendours of Georgian Edinburgh is the **New Town Conservation Committee** (*13A Dundas Street*).

When exploring Georgian Edinburgh look for the many decorative details which give the New Town so much of its cha-racter. The cast-iron work shows great variety of design (Heriot Row and Abercromby Place). Stretches of balcony spanning the frontages (Windsor Street and Atholl Crescent) alternate with window guards; the serried ranks of railings crested with finials are punctuated by lamp standards, brackets and extinguishers or link horns (Charlotte Square, York Place and Melville Street).

■ Charlotte Square to the east end of Princes Street

Charlotte Square*** – Following allegations of piecemeal development of the New Town scheme in its early stages, **Robert Adam** was commissioned in 1791 to design what is now the New Town's most splendid square. Elegant frontages of a unified design frame the garden with a central equestrian statue of **Prince Albert** by Steell. The **north side** is a grand civic achievement where the vertical lines of the advanced central and end blocks are counterbalanced by the rusticated ground floor. The lines of straight-headed windows, round-headed doorway fanlights and occasional Venetian windows are happily juxtaposed. Note the wrought-iron railings, lamp holders, extinguishers and foot scrapers. The **centrepiece** comprises the headquarters of the National Trust for Scotland (no 5),

Bute House (no 6), the official residence of the Secretary of State for Scotland and no 7, **The Georgian House**★. The lower floors have been entirely refurbished by the NTS as a typical Georgian home of the period from 1790 to 1810. Some of the delights include the cheese waggon, rare wine rinsing glasses, lovely Scottish sideboard, moreen hangings, tea table and well equipped kitchen and wine cellar. An introduction to Georgian Edinburgh is provided in one of the basement rooms (two videos: 33min).

A mirror image of the north side of the square, the south side has been comprehensively restored in as authentic a manner as possible by the National Trust.

On the west side, St George's Church (1811-14) by Robert Reid provides the focal point for George Street and is now converted into the National Archives of Scotland annexe, **West Register House**. There is a permanent historical exhibition inside.

Famous residents included Lord Cockburn at no 14, Lord Lister (no 9) and Douglas Haig (no 24).

George Street – The principal street of Craig's plan is closed at either end by Charlotte and St Andrew Squares; it is 0.5mi/800m in length and 115ft/35m wide. Many of the houses of this originally residential street are now converted into banks, offices and shops.

Statues punctuate the street intersections – Dr Chalmers by Steell at Castle Street; Pitt by Chantrey at Frederick Street and George IV also by Chantrey at Hanover Street – each of which has good views away to the Forth or down to Princes Street Gardens with the castle and Old Town as backdrop. Note in particular the **view** surveyed by George IV from his pedestal, with the successive landmarks perfectly positioned Royal Scottish Academy, National Gallery, Assembly Hall and spire of the former Tolbooth Kirk.

Towards the east end are the **Assembly Rooms** (no 54) built in 1784; the pedimented portico was a later addition. This was Edinburgh's fifth such institution, but the first in the New Town. Paradoxically it was the more spacious apartments of the New Town dwellings which caused the demise of the rooms as a centre for regular social gatherings. Started in 1784, they were opened three years later during Burns' first visit to the capital. It was here that Scott proclaimed his authorship of the *Waverley Novels*. This fine suite of rooms, with the Music Hall behind, is a magnificent setting for public functions.

St Andrew and St George Church (1785), with its towering spire, was intended to close the George Street vista at the St Andrew Square end, but Dundas beat the planners to it. The church was the scene of the 1843 Disruption when a group of ministers led by Dr Chalmers walked out of the church over the issue of patronage, and formed the Free Church of Scotland.

Scottish National Portrait Gallery* – *1 Queen Street.* In the best Victorian tradition a munificent donation by the proprietor of *The Scotsman* provided a building for the illustration of Scottish history. Rowand Anderson designed an Italianate Gothic, statue-decorated building to house the portrait collection founded in 1882. In 1890-91 the Antiquarian Society moved in from its premises in the Mound.

The initial aim of the National Portrait Gallery was to "illustrate Scottish history by likeness of the chief actors in it". Many of the portraits of persons of historic interest are masterpieces of portraiture. Scottish exponents of this tradition include the 16C George Jamesone *(self-portrait)*, John Michael Wright, the 18C masters, Ramsay *(David Hume* the companion portrait to the one of J J Rousseau) and Raeburn *(Scott).* In addition there are canvases by Wissing, Lely, Gainsborough,

Lawrence... Some of the chief actors portrayed are royalty *(Mary, Queen of Scots, Lord Darnley, James VI, Charles I, Elizabeth of Bohemia and James VII)*; statesmen formal and fine *(1st Earl of Dunfermline and Duke of Lauderdale)*; 18C to 19C politicians *(Kier Hardie, Ramsay MacDonald and W E Gladstone)*; literary figures *(Drummond of Hawthornden, Burns, Scott, Byron, Carlyle, Stevenson and Barrie).*

St Andrew Square – Here **Henry Dundas**, Viscount Melville, better known as King Harry the Ninth for his management of Scottish affairs between 1782 and 1805, still dominates from his fluted column (150ft/46m high). The square, the home of banks and insurance companies, has none of the unified elegance of its counterpart, Charlotte Square, but has individual buildings of charm and splendour. On the north side nos 21 to 26 are examples of the vernacular classical style of the first phase of New Town development. **Buchan House** (nos 21, 22) perpetuates the name of the eccentric 11th Earl of Buchan (1742-1829), founder of the Society of Antiquaries and regular correspondent of George III whom he addressed as Cousin.

No 26, with its elegant touches, was by Adam's chief rival, Sir William Chambers, who was also responsible for the magnificent mansion on the east side. **Dundas House*** was built (1772-74) for Sir Laurence Dundas on what was originally intended to be a church site. Well set back, this three-storey mansion is adorned with a projecting three-bay pilastered emblazoned, pedimented central section and a frieze at roof level. Step inside to see the splendours of the original entrance hall where capitals and roof bosses are highlighted in gold leaf. The building was purchased by the Royal Bank of Scotland in 1825 and the domed banking hall was added in 1858. In front of the bank stand the soldier 4th Earl of Hopetoun and his horse. Of the two symmetrical pavilions flanking the mansion no 35 to the north, when built in 1768, was the earliest house in the square. The façade of no 38, another bank, is strikingly ornate with Corinthian columns rising through two floors and each crowned by a statue. The philosopher David Hume (1711-76) was among the first of Edinburgh's notables to move in 1771 to a New Town house in St David Street, named after him.

West Register Street leads past the literary pub **Café Royal** with its oyster bar, to **New Register House** fronted by fine wrought-iron gates and crowned gateposts indicating the offices of the Court of Lord Lyon with his Heralds and Pursuivants.

Robert Louis Stevenson (1850-94)

A plaque inscribed with a verse of *The Lamplighter*, a poem for children, marks the site of Stevenson's childhood home at 17 Heriot Row *(private property)* in the New Town. He is famous for adventure stories such as *Treasure Island* and *Kidnapped* which have enthralled children through the years, and for his more sombre tale *Dr Jekyll and Mr Hyde* which is set in the old town.

The Lord Lyon King of Arms regulates all Scottish armorial matters, adjudicates upon Chiefship of clans, conducts and executes Royal Proclamations and state and public ceremonials of all descriptions in Scotland.

The east end of Princes Street is now dominated by Robert Adam's splendid frontage of **General Register House** (1774-1822) headquarters of the National Archives of Scotland. With the projecting pedimented portico and end pavilions crowned by cupolas, it makes a suitably gracious focal point for North Bridge. Changing exhibitions are mounted in the front hall. Look through into the splendid domed hall with its characteristic Adam motifs.

At pavement level is Steell's equestrian **statue of Wellington**.

The **General Post Office** stands on the site of the Theatre Royal built in 1768, as one of the first buildings in the New Town. During its heyday when Scott was a trustee, famous names such as Sarah Siddons and John Kemble performed here. The theatre closed in 1859 and was burnt down in 1946. Opposite is the Balmoral Hotel with its famous clock tower landmark, and clock reputedly always two minutes fast.

He took many trips abroad to warmer climes for health reasons including two to France which inspired him to write *An Inland Voyage* (1878) and *Travels with a Donkey in the Cévennes* (1879). ■

PRINCES STREET AND GARDENS

Princes Street – Edinburgh's prime shopping street was originally totally residential. Single sided, the street marked the southern extension of the New Town. The 1770s town houses were modest but appreciated for the open view across the valley, which later became a private garden for residents. Following the laying of the railway (1845-46), commercial development slowly took over. Today Victorian and modern shops and hotels stand side by side. A few like Jenners are a reminder of the opulent emporiums and establishments that once lined the street.

Princes Street Gardens – The Nor'Loch Valley was infilled during New Town excavation work and later laid out as private gardens for residents. Lord Cockburn was the instigator of the Act of Parliament which safeguarded the south side of Princes Street from further development. With the coming of the railways, shops and hotels replaced houses and in 1876 the gardens were opened to the public. Today the gardens with their greenery, welcome benches and many monuments provide a pleasant respite from the milling crowd in Princes Street.

★Scott Monument – This pinnacled monument dominating Princes Street is one of Edinburgh's most familiar landmarks. Following Scott's death in 1832, a successful public appeal was launched. Much controversy ensued as to the site and nature of the monument however the foundation stone was laid in 1840. The neo-Gothic spire (200ft/61m tall) was designed by a joiner and draughtsman, **George Meikle Kemp**, who died before its completion. Steell's Carrara marble statue of Scott and his dog Maida is accompanied by 64 statuettes of characters from his novels (in the niches) and the heads of 16 Scottish poets (on the capitals). The monument became a major attraction. For the agile, four viewing platforms *(287 steps)* give good **views★** of central Edinburgh. The first floor room has a display on the designer and the construction.

Dividing Princes Street Gardens into East and West are two imposing Classical buildings on the left:

the National Gallery and the Royal Scottish Academy.

National Gallery of Scotland★★ – The nucleus of the Gallery was formed by the Royal Institution's collection, later expanded by bequests and purchasing. Playfair designed (1850-57) the imposing Classical building to house the works. The elegant octagonal rooms with their connecting arches have been tastefully refurbished. A more intimate atmosphere has been achieved and the paintings, displayed chronologically, are complemented by appropriate period furniture and sculpture. *Start with Room 1 on the upper floor by taking the staircase opposite the main entrance.*

The Early Northern and Early Italian holdings include the *Trinity Altarpiece* (c 1470s) by Van der Goes, a unique example of pre-Reformation art commissioned for Edinburgh's now demolished Collegiate Church of the Holy Trinity. Open, the panels represent James III and

Margaret of Denmark with patron saints. *The Three Legends of St Nicholas* by Gerard David shows scenes from the life of St Nicholas of Myra, more commonly known as Santa Claus. Early Italian works introduce one of the principal figures of the period, Raphael with his gentle *Bridgewater Madonna* and an excellent example of High Renaissance portraiture by his contemporary, Andrea del Sarto *(Portrait of the Artist's Friend)*.

Downstairs, **Galleries I** and **II** introduce the principal figures of early-16C Venetian painting: Jacopo Bassano with the colourful *Adoration of the Kings* and Titian with his religious composition *The Three Ages of Man.* Two examples of Titian's

Sir Walter Scott Monument

late style of mythological painting (1550s) display all the painterly qualities of Venetian art: *Diana and Actaeon* and *Diana and Calisto* show a freedom of brushwork and masterly handling of colour and paint. Compare them with the works of other major artists of the second generation of 16C painters: Bassano, Tintoretto's *The Deposition of Christ*, characteristic of his summary style, and Veronese (*Mars and Venus, St Anthony Abbot*) who remained first and foremost a colourist.

Gallery III, arranged as a Kunstkammer, displays a number of miscellaneous 16C and 17C European Cabinet Pictures (Cranach, Holbein, Clouet, Rubens and Avercamp). **Gallery IV** gathers together 17C works by Poussin (*The Mystic Marriage of St Catherine*), Claude Lorrain (*Landscape with Apollo and the Muses*), El Greco (*The Saviour of the World* with its particular colouring, elongation and spiritual power and *Fable* on a rare secular theme), as well as an early work by Velazquez (*An Old Woman Cooking Eggs*).

Poussin's admirable *Seven Sacraments* are enhanced by the gracious setting of **Gallery V**. Note how the marble floor echoes the one in the *Confirmation*. Poussin undertook this second series of formal classical compositions for a Parisian friend, Chantelou.

The diversity of 17C Dutch art is well represented in **Galleries VI, VII** and **IX**. Jan Weenix specialises in large hunting scenes. Cuyp's *View of the Valkhof, Nijmegen* introduces interesting light effects and Koninck's *Onset of a Storm* combines imaginary views with natural scenery. Alongside, the portraits of Frans Hals display a vitality and realism which make them second only to those of Rembrandt represented by his *Self-Portrait Aged 51*, where the use of chiaroscuro focuses attention on the face. In the next gallery (**VII**), landscapes by the specialists Ruisdael and Hobbema hang with Philip Koninck's large-scale *Extensive Landscape* (1666) with a characteristic high viewpoint.

Gallery IX (17C Flemish and Dutch painting) contains canvases by the 17C master Rubens. The swirling movement of his *Feast of Herod*, a large banqueting scene full of colour and realism, contrasts with the staid formalism of Van Dyck's *The Lomellini Family*. Vermeer's early work *Christ in the House of Martha and Mary* shows Mary in an attentive mood.

The principal figures of 18C British art are introduced in **Gallery X**: Gainsborough (*The Hon Mrs Graham, Mrs Hamilton Nisbet*), Reynolds (*Ladies Waldegrave*), Romney, Raeburn and Lawrence. Other 18C schools are represented by three pastoral scenes of joyful frivolity by France's foremost Rococo painter, François Boucher, the last exponent of the Venetian Renaissance tradition; G B Tiepolo's *The Finding of Moses*; and Gavin Hamilton, a pioneer in neo-Classicism (*Achilles mourning the Death of Patroclus*).

19C British and American works (**Gallery XI**) include landscapes by Turner (*Somer Hill, Tunbridge*), Constable (*Vale of Dedham*), Ward (*The Eildon Hills and the Tweed, Melrose Abbey*) and the American, Church (*Niagara Falls*). Next door in **Gallery XII** hang Sir Benjamin West's gigantic work *Alexander III of Scotland rescued from the fury*

Princes Street Gardens

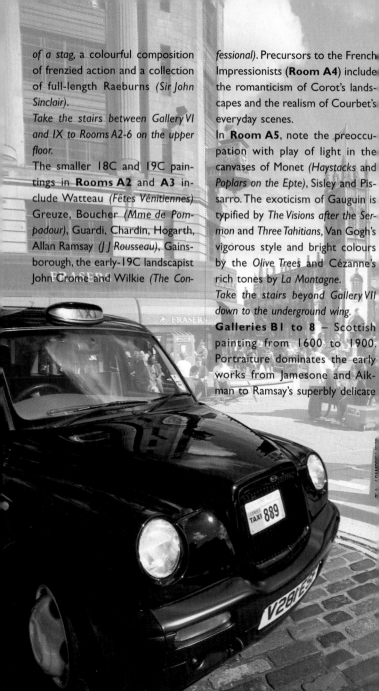

of a stag, a colourful composition of frenzied action and a collection of full-length Raeburns *(Sir John Sinclair)*.

Take the stairs between Gallery VI and IX to Rooms A2-6 on the upper floor.

The smaller 18C and 19C paintings in **Rooms A2** and **A3** include Watteau *(Fêtes Vénitiennes)* Greuze, Boucher *(Mme de Pompadour)*, Guardi, Chardin, Hogarth, Allan Ramsay *(J J Rousseau)*, Gainsborough, the early-19C landscapist John Crome and Wilkie *(The Con-*

fessional). Precursors to the French Impressionists **(Room A4)** include the romanticism of Corot's landscapes and the realism of Courbet's everyday scenes.

In **Room A5**, note the preoccupation with play of light in the canvases of Monet *(Haystacks* and *Poplars on the Epte)*, Sisley and Pissarro. The exoticism of Gauguin is typified by *The Visions after the Sermon* and *Three Tahitians*, Van Gogh's vigorous style and bright colours by the *Olive Trees* and Cézanne's rich tones by *La Montagne*.

Take the stairs beyond Gallery VII down to the underground wing.

Galleries B1 to 8 – Scottish painting from 1600 to 1900. Portraiture dominates the early works from Jamesone and Aikman to Ramsay's superbly delicate portraits of women. Beyond are numerous examples of Raeburn's works including a *self-portrait* and *The Reverend Robert Walker Skating on Duddingston Loch*. David Wilkie knew great popularity in his time for his realistic Scottish scenes, *Distraining for Rent, The Letter of Introduction* and his first important work *Pitlessie Fair*. *The Gentle Shepherd* is inspired by Ramsay's poem. Nasmyth's *Edinburgh Castle and the Nor'Loch, The Distant View of Stirling* are soft and atmospheric compositions. William Dyce, precursor of the Pre-Raphaelites, specialised in religious scenes and landscapes (*St Catherine, Christ as the Man of Sorrows*). *Francesca da Rimini* illustrates an episode of Dante's Inferno. *Quarrel and Reconciliation* and *Dawn: Luther* are imaginative works by Paton. *The Porteous Mob* by J Drummond is based on an historical episode described in Scott's *Heart of Midlothian*.

McTaggart excelled in landscapes (*The Storm, The Young Fishers*) where bold brushwork and dramatic light effects introduced a sense of realism. The follow-up movement was the Glasgow School (*see Index*) to which Guthrie and EA Hornel both belonged.

Taxi at the West End

Royal Scottish Academy – The Academy was custom built by William Playfair in 1826 to grace the north end of the Mound and counterbalance the Bank of Scotland's imposing building at the south end. From her perch above the portico, Steell's Queen Victoria looks up Hanover Street towards her uncle, George IV. The initial rivalry between Institution and Academy ended when the latter became royal in 1838. The Royal Scottish Academy, composed of 60 members of whom 30 are Academicians and the others associates, organises exhibitions throughout the year.

The Mound – The drained Nor'Loch area was initially crossed by stepping stones laid by an enterprising Lawnmarket clothier as a short cut for his New Town clients. Later, excavated earth from New Town building sites was used to build up the Mound (1781-1805) as it stands today.

Beyond, in West Princes Street Gardens are the **floral clock** composed of 20 000 annuals, the bandstand, a centre for a full programme of open-air entertainment in summer, and statues of the poet Allan Ramsay (east end) and the discoverer of chloroform Sir James Y Simpson. ∎

CALTON HILL

See city plan

At the east end of Princes Street rises Calton Hill (328ft/100m) with that familiar skyline of Classical monuments which gave rise to the name, "Edinburgh's acropolis". Another remnant of volcanic activity, Calton Hill (22 acres/9ha) was left undeveloped when the New Town was being built.

The James Craig **Observatory** was the initial building and development continued after 1815 when the ravine to the east of Princes Street had been crossed by Regent Bridge. The flanking porticoes and Classical façades of **Waterloo Place** provide a formal entry, framing Calton Hill in the distance.

On the right, **St Andrew's House**), the former administrative centre of Scotland, stands on the site of two prisons, built to relieve the Old Tolbooth.

Calton Hill – *Access by stairs from Waterloo Place (Regent Road) or by a narrow road, suitable for cars, leading off to the left opposite St Andrew's House.* The most striking monument is the 12-columned portico of the **National Monument** to commemorate Scots who died in the Napoleonic Wars. It was intended as a replica of the Parthenon but construction was stopped by lack of funds. The next in a clockwise direction and tallest is the **Nelson Monument** a tiered circular tower (106ft/32m tall) to the victor of Trafalgar. The viewing gallery *(143 steps)* provides a magnificent **panorama***** of Edinburgh: up

Beltane Fire Festival

Since 1988 a festival marking the end of winter is held every year on Calton Hill. Until the beginning of the 20C this celebration, which is derived from an old Celtic tradition, took place on the site of St Anthony's Well on the eve of 1 May.

The main protagonists of this festival are: the May Queen and her retinue, a team of fighters known as the White Women, the Green Man and the Blue Man. Others such as the Red Men holding aloft torches process around a large bonfire to the sound of drums.

Princes Street, from the castle down the spine of the Royal Mile past the Canongate Church, to Holyroodhouse with Arthur's Seat in the background.

The circular Greek **temple** is Playfair's monument to Dugald Stewart, Professor of Moral Philosophy. The walled enclosure has at its southwest corner James Craig's 18C Old Observatory which was subsequently replaced by Playfair's building (1818) in the centre, itself superseded by a new Observatory on Blackford Hill (*see Royal Observatory below*). At the southeast corner is another Playfair monument, this time to his uncle, the mathematician and natural philosopher, John Playfair.

Edinburgh Experience – The Old Observatory is the venue for an exciting audio-visual presentation of Edinburgh's rich history.

Regent Road – The **Royal High School** with its imposing co-lumned, pedimented and porticoed façade was designed by a former pupil Thomas Hamilton from 1825 to 1829. The oval debating chamber is now used by Scottish MPs when debating Scottish affairs.

Beyond, to the right of the road, is the Greek temple to Robert Burns by the architect of the Royal High School.

Branch left to follow the contour of Calton Hill and the elegant sweep of **Regent** (1825), **Calton** (1820s-1860) and **Royal Terraces** (1821-60). William Playfair designed a residential area; here also are many of the attractive architectural and ironwork features typical of the New Town. The communal garden (*private*) behind was laid out by Joseph Paxton. ■

H. Wood, D. Corrance & M. Alexander and ELTB

View from Calton Hill

Royal Botanic Garden★★★ – *1mi/ 1.5km from the city centre by Broughton Street* **(BY 6)**. *Car parking available near the west gate in Arboretum Road.* The 70 acres of the Royal Botanic Garden are a refreshing haven for those weary of the city bustle. It is a pleasure to stroll through the splendid grounds which offer many treasures for the initiated.

Origins – In the late 17C when Edinburgh was emerging as a centre for medical studies, a physic garden was established (1670) by Dr Robert Sibbald, first Professor of Medicine at Edinburgh University, and Dr Robert Balfour, another eminent physician. The original plot was situated near Holyrood Abbey. In 1676 these gentlemen acquired land near Trinity Hospital – on the present site of Waverley Station – appointing James Sutherland as Intendant. An intermediary move to Leith Walk followed before the final one in c 1820 to a mere 14 acres on the present site. A later extension included Inverleith House and its policies.

Today – The garden, glasshouses and herbarium, with its vast collection of preserved plant specimens, are the working basis

for research, the main role of the garden. Edinburgh's specialisation in rhododendrons owes much to such dedicated collectors as George Forrest.

Garden and buildings – The **rhododendrons** are a major attraction. The modernistic Exhibition Plant Houses (1967) provide unimpeded interiors where winding paths lead through a series of landscaped presentations, a pleasant alternative to serried ranks of pots so normally associated with glasshouses. The Exhibition Hall is devoted to changing displays on various aspects of botany. The Tropical (1834) and Temperate (1858) Palm Houses have an altogether more traditional and imposing architectural style. High in the centre of the gardens stands 18C **Inverleith House**, formerly the repository for the collection of modern art *(see below)*. From beyond the lawn a view indicator pinpoints Edinburgh's well-known landmarks.

Royal Yacht Britannia★ – *In the port of Leith, 2mi/3km north of the city centre via Leith Walk.* The Royal Yacht Britannia was launched from a Clydebank shipyard in April 1953. By the time she was decommissioned in December 1997, this symbol of post-Imperial royalty had sailed more than a million miles, carrying Queen Elizabeth II and her family on nearly 1 000 official visits to countries around the world.

The roles Britannia played, from floating palace to venue for the promotion of British exports, are explained in a visitor centre, spacious enough to contain a royal barge afloat in a tank of water. Once aboard, visitors can follow a trail through royal apartments, crew's quarters, bridge and wheelhouse, and engine room. Designed by Sir Hugh Casson in close consultation with the Queen and Prince Philip, the royal apartments have a cool but comfortable style, a subtle combination of country house luxury and shipboard practicality.

The audio tour brings the ship's past alive, explaining the meticulous arrangements for formal dining as well as the rules for the boisterous game of "wombat tennis" played by officers in the wardroom.

St Mary's Episcopal Cathedral – *Enter from Palmerston Place.* The cathedral was built for the Episcopalian diocese of Edinburgh by George Gilbert Scott in the 1870s. Vast and ambitious, even for the Victorians, the cathedral stands as a testament of faith. The exterior is dominated by the three spires. The two west front ones are later (1917) additions.

Inside, the quality of Victorian craftsmanship is evident everywhere. Note the pelican lectern, the Robert Lorimer designed rood and the reredos of the high altar.

The latter by the architect's son, J Aldrid Scott, depicts in the side niches St Margaret and St Columba, two leading influences in the early Scottish Church.

In the grounds stand the 17C Old Coates House (now a Theological Institute) and the Song School famous for its restored **murals**, painted by Phoebe Anna Traquair (1888-92) on the theme of "Benedicite omnia opera".

Scottish National Gallery of Modern Art* – *Belford Road*. The Scottish National Gallery of Modern Art is situated in large wooded grounds, on the western edge of the New Town, which provide a fine setting for sculptures by Bourdelle, Epstein, Hepworth, Moore and Rickey. The Gallery is housed in an imposing neo-Classical building, the former John Watson's School.

The collection has two emphases: international and Scottish art of the 20C. If not fully comprehensive in its international collection, it does nevertheless have fine examples of most of the main artists and movements: the Nabis and Fauvism (Vuillard, Bonnard, Matisse, Derain, Rouault), German Expressionism (Kirchner, Nolde, Jawlensky, Kokoschka, Dix), Cubism and its derivatives (Braque, Picasso, Léger, Delaunay, Lipchitz), Russian Primitivism and Abstract Art (Gontcharova, Larionov, Popova), Abstraction (Moholy-Nagy, Mondrian, Schwitters, Nicholson), School of Paris (De Staël, Balthus, Dubuffet, Soulages, Riopelle, Tápies, Appel, Picasso), Nouveau Réalisme (César, Arman, Tinguely), St Ives School (Nicholson, Hepworth, Lanyon, Hilton), Pop Art (Lichtenstein, Hockney, Hamilton, Paolozzi, Tilson, Kitaj), Minimal Art (Lewitt, Judd, Flavin). The **Scottish Collection** is rich and comprehensive. It has particularly good holdings of the work of the Scottish Colourists (Peploe, Cadell, Hunter, Fergusson) and the Edinburgh School (Gillies, Maxwell, McTaggart and Redpath).

Dean Gallery* – *Belford Road, opposite Gallery of Modern Art*. Built in 1833 as an orphanage, this imposing and idiosyncratic building by the Greek Revival architect Thomas Hamilton makes a surprisingly suitable setting for the National Gallery's specialist collections of contemporary art, with imaginatively redesigned interiors by Terry Farrell.

The **Dada** and **Surrealist** holdings, based on the collections of Sir Roland Penrose and Gabrielle Keiller, include works by Ernst, Dalí, de Chirico, Magritte, Schwitters, Miró, Picasso, Magritte, Delvaux, Tristram Hillier and Henry Moore. Masks, skulls, other *objets trouvés* and the contents of Penrose's cabinet of curiosities help create the bizarre atmosphere favoured by the Surrealists.

The Paolozzi Gift consists of a large number of works by the Edinburgh-born sculptor **Eduardo Paolozzi** (1924-), among them the gigantic stainless steel *Vulcan* rising through two floors in the centre of the building. Beyond a room containing a number of the artist's characteristic figures which seem to have survived some unimaginable Armageddon is a reconstruction of Paolozzi's fascinatingly crammed studio.

Temporary exhibitions are held on the upper floor.

Edinburgh Zoo★★ – *3mi/5km from the city centre, on the main Edinburgh – Glasgow road, A 8.* The 80-acre Scottish National Zoological Park is attractively set on the south slope of Corstorphine Hill. Barless and sometimes glassless enclosures for many of the species allow the visitor better views of the animals and their antics. The tables are turned as the orang-utans and chimpanzees, from their pole-top perch and climbing apparatus, have grandstand views of the public. The famous Edinburgh penguin collection (a colony of 30 Kings and 100 Gentoes) is the number one attraction with their daily **Penguin Parade.**

In addition to the usual animals, make a point of looking for some of the native species: the wild cat, shy pine martens or golden eagle. The **view** from the hilltop (510ft/ 155m; *view indicator*) shows the sprawl of Edinburgh and from the Pentlands to the south, right round to the mountains of Loch Lomond.

Lauriston Castle – *5mi/8km from the city centre by A 90 and Cramond Road South.* The 16C tower house was built by Sir Archibald Napier, father of the inventor of logarithms. **John Law** (1671-1729), financier and France's Comptroller General of Finances, spent some of his early years here. Greatly extended in the 19C and refurbished in the early 20C, the house today is an example of a gracious Edwardian home. Of particular interest are some of the very fine pieces of furniture (18C English and Continental and 20C reproductions), the unusual wool "mosaics" and collection of Blue John ware. Tapestries and a large collection of prints adorn the walls. Do not miss the cases of James Tassie's (1735-99) casts of his famous intaglios.

Edinburgh Zoo

Scottish Agricultural Museum *
– *Ingliston. 7mil/11km west by A 8.*
The museum gives an informative
and well documented account
of Scotland's rural past. On the
ground floor, the seasonal activities
from ploughing to harvesting are
presented using a combination of
exhibits, backed up by explanatory
texts and photographs. In sharp
contrast to the sophisticated ma-
chinery of today, the implements of
the past like the Shetland delling
spade, the back harrow, the sickle
and scythe are reminders of the
sheer physical labour involved in
farming of earlier times.

Other exhibits evoke scenes
which are now a thing of the
past: the teams of working horses,
the harvests with binders, stooks
and cornyards of neatly thatched
stacks and the activity of the travelling mill. The authentic details of
the house interiors, in particular
the bothy, are noteworthy. ■

SOUTHERN SUBURBS

The **Royal Observatory (Visitor Centre)** – *3mi/5km from the city centre by A 7.* The observatory was transferred to Blackford Hill in 1896 to escape "the smokiness of the air" of Calton Hill. The **visitor centre** (East Tower) introduces the public to the history of the present observatory and the anatomy of a modern observatory.

The **West Tower** is occupied by an 16in/40cm Schmidt telescope *(no longer in active use)* while boards on the walls of the tower describe the role of the UK 48in/1.2m Schmidt telescope in Australia which is used for photographic observations of large areas of the sky.

The flat roof beyond provides a good **view★** of urban Edinburgh from the Bass Rock in the east, away to Fife and the Lomond Hills on the horizon. Calton Hill, the original observatory site, is diminutive but distinguishable.

The exhibition in the **Rooftop Gallery** covers the history of early observational astronomy and the development of the astronomical telescope, including the role of Scotland's own James Gregory *(see Index)*. Installed in the **East Tower** is the 36in/91cm telescope (1930) which ranks as Scotland's largest.

Craigmillar Castle★ – *3mi/5km southeast by St Leonard's Street and A 68.* Dramatically set on an eminence, Craigmillar is impressive for its show of strength and seeming impregnability. The 14C tower house rises massively above two successive curtain walls. The outer wall encloses a courtyard in front and gardens on either side, in all a total area of over 1 acre. The inner curtain built in 1427 is quartered with round towers, pierced by gunloops and topped by attractive oversailing machicolated parapets. Above the inner gate is the Preston family coat of arms. Straight ahead stands the L-shaped **tower house**, now flanked by and linked to the later east (15C) and west ranges (16C-17C). The **Great Hall** at first floor level is a grand apartment with a magnificent hooded fireplace and three windows with stone benches lining the embrasures. Climb to the top to get a view down over the other buildings and fully appreciate the strategic excellence of the layout.

Note the dovecot in the northeast corner of the outer wall and the P-shaped fish pond in the field to the south.

It was here that Mary, Queen of Scots sought refuge after the murder of Rizzio *(see Index)* and here that the treacherous plot for the murder of Darnley was conceived.

Midlothian Ski Centre – *Hillend, off A 702.* The centre, on the north slopes of the Pentland Hills, opened in 1965. The artificial ski slopes operate throughout the year and cater for skiers of all abilities. Visitors can take the ski lift up to the top station (*view indicator and binoculars*) which offers a magnificent **panorama**** of Edinburgh and its southern suburbs with, on the horizon, Ben Lomond, round to Cockenzie Power Station, North Berwick Law, Traprain and the Cheviots.

Castlelaw Hill Fort – *Off A 702. Take the road to the left up to Castlelaw farm and the car park. The fort is on a Ministry of Defence Range; obey instructions given by flag or lamps.*

The fort, consisting of concentric banks and ditches, is set on the summit of Castle Knowe on the southeasterly slopes of the Pentland Hills. The earth house built into the inner ditch consists of a gallery (56ft/17m long) with a beehive chamber (11ft/3m in diameter) off to the right. The floors are of rock while the walls are faced with masonry.

Malleny Garden – *Balerno off A 70.* Situated on the southern bank of the Water of Leith, the 17C house (private) stands on the site of a royal hunting lodge and has an elegant early-19C wing to the east. There is an attractive woodland garden. ■

PRACTICAL INFORMATION

■ Planning a trip ■

Tourist Information Offices

Visit Scotland is Scotland's national tourist board. Their head office is at 23 Ravelston Terrace, Edinburgh EH4 3EU ☎ 0131 332 2433 fax 0131 459 2434 www.visitscotland.com

Once you get to Edinburgh, the Edinburgh & Scotland Information Centre, above Waverley Station, 3 Princes Street, is a good place to begin your visit. As well as general information, they also deal with accommodation reservations, tours, excursions, coach tickets, theatres and Scottish entertainment. Try to go first thing in the morning as it gets very busy.

The centre's opening hours are: winter, Mon-Wed 9am-5pm, Thu-Sat 9am-6/7pm, Sun 10am-5/6pm; summer, Mon-Sat 9am-7pm, Sun 10am-7pm. These are extended during the Festival. ☎ 0131 473 3800 fax 0131 473 3881 www.edinburgh.org

For booking accommodation in advance, e-mail: centres@eltb.org

The other Edinburgh office is at the airport (open daily all year) ☎ 0131 333 1000 fax 0131 335 3576.

Representatives of the tourist office also take to the streets wearing distinctive tartan jackets or bright yellow waterproofs; they can be seen at major arrival points and areas of interest, including the Royal Mile, Waverley Bridge and Princes Street.

Special Needs

For guides to facilities and accommodation services contact RADAR, 12 City Forum, 250 City Road, London EC1V 8AF ☎ (202) 7250 3222; or the Holiday Care Service, 2 Old Bank Chambers, Station Road, Horley, Surrey RH6 9HW ☎ (01293) 774 535.

In Edinburgh, contact the Lothian Coalition of Disabled People, Norton Park, 57 Albion Road, Edinburgh EH7 5QY ☎ 0131 475 2360 fax 0131 475 2392, who publish the free Access Guide to Edinburgh.

■ Getting there ■

By Air

Edinburgh Airport is 12km (8 miles) west of the city and handles domestic and international flights. British Airways is the national carrier and flies regularly to Edinburgh from Heathrow, as does British Midland which is usually cheaper. Easyjet flies from Luton. Flight time from London is about an hour.

A special Airlink 100 bus service runs every 10 minutes during the day between the airport and city centre (Waverley Bridge) and takes around 25 minutes. Buy your tickets on board. Taxis are available but are expensive, costing around £15 to Princes Street.

By Train

Edinburgh has two main railway stations: **Waverley** and **Haymarket**. Great North Eastern Railway (GNER) services the east coast of mainland Britain, with a fast, comfortable, efficient service from London, King's Cross to Edinburgh (Waverley Station) taking around 4 hours. Virgin Trains run from London (Euston Station) to Edinburgh (Haymarket Station) but with a change at Birmingham. The total journey time is around 5 1/2 to 6 hours. From Haymarket to the west end of Princes Street is a 10-minute walk (bus no 3, 3A, 12 or 25).

By Coach

National Express operates a regular service between the major towns in the UK and Edinburgh. Special discount tickets available: contact local National Express agents or

National Express – www.gobycoach.com

Ensign Court, 4 Vicarage Road, Edgbaston, Birmingham B15 3ES

☎ 08705 80 80 80.

■ Getting around ■

Edinburgh is a compact city and the quickest way to get about the centre is often to walk. Consider a car only for touring outside the city.

Buses

The public bus service is run by several operators, of whom the biggest is Lothian Regional Transport (LRT). LRT buses (maroon and white) require the correct money, though some of the other operators do give change. Daysaver tickets (£2.20 for a day's unlimited travel) will generally make a saving after more than two journeys, and also save you the hassle of handling cash. They are sold on board or at Travelshops. Note, however, that they are not transferable between different bus companies. A weekly, fortnightly or monthly Ridacard ticket is a bargain, if you are going to make several regular LRT trips. To get one you will have to take along a passport photo to one of their Travelshops (at Hanover Street and Waverley Bridge). Another option is the Touristcard (2-7 days) which costs more but also includes the Edinburgh Classic (sightseeing) Tour and gives discounts on attractions and restaurants.

Nightbuses run from around midnight to 4am.

For all bus enquiries pick up a free route map from the tourist office, call into a Travelshop, or call ☎ 0800 232323.

Taxis

These can be pre-booked, taken from a taxi rank or hailed on the street. The licensed black taxi cabs work on the meter and are expensive. Unlicensed 'minicabs', which are any other form of taxi, are cheaper and generally agree the fare in advance but get a recommendation to make sure you have an honest and reputable driver. Look in the local directory for a full list of numbers.

Bicycles

Bicycle hire is not recommended for inexperienced cyclists as city centre traffic can be heavy, and the cobbles and hills can make cycling hard work. There is, however, a good network of cycle paths; an old railway line has been converted to a safe flat cycle route near Stockbridge; The Water of Leith Walkway is another pleasant traffic-free option, albeit rather narrow in parts.

Car Rental/Hire

The most flexible way of exploring the outskirts of the city is by car. There are numerous car hire agencies, both at the airport and in town. The rates are among the highest in Europe but local firms are usually significantly cheaper than international operators. A full list of car hire firms is available from the Tourist Information Office, or in Yellow Pages.

■ Sightseeing ■

Tours

There are all sorts of walking tours and bus tours within and outside the city. For an overview take an open-top hop-bus tour with commentary which allows you to hop on and off at will: Guide Friday (133-135 Canongate, Royal Mile ☎ 0131 556 2244) or Edinburgh Tour – City Sightseeing (☎ 0131 555 6363) – buses for both depart from Waverley Bridge.

Typically Edinburgh tours that will get you into the spirit of the city, in more ways than one, include the McEwans 80/- Literary Pub Tour or one of the city's many ghost tours.

For details of all of these and of coach tours which take you to places of interest outside Edinburgh, enquire at the main tourist office.

Maps and Guidebooks

The Michelin Red Guide Great Britain and Ireland contains detailed information on hotels and restaurants throughout Scotland, including Edinburgh. The Michelin Green Guide Scotland has information on the main sights and attractions in Edinburgh, detailed street maps of the city and also includes other towns and attractions you may visit as excursions from Edinburgh. The Michelin Road Map 501 Scotland (1:400 000) will help with route-planning. If you are staying for only a few days and don't want to venture out of the centre, the excellent Edinburgh Navigator City Centre Pocket Map (free from the Waverley Tourist Information Office) is perfectly adequate. Also ask at the tourist office for a bus map.

■ Shopping ■

Princes Street, the busy main shopping street, is lined with quality stores such as Jenners, a reminder of more elegant times, and popular high-street names – John Lewis (St James Shopping Centre), Marks and Spencer and Boots. George Street is lined with trendy shops (Harvey Nichols, Karen Millen).

Fashion boutiques and music shops are to be found in Rose Street (parallel to Princes Street). Antique shops are mainly in the area around the Royal Mile, Victoria Street and Grassmarket in the Old Town and in Dundas and Thistle Streets in the New Town.

Quality garments in tweed, tartan, cashmere and wool are sold in Jenners, Burberrys, the Scotch House, Romanes Patterson (Princes Street) and Kinloch Anderson. The Cashmere Store in the Royal Mile and Kinloch Anderson's Retail Shop on the corner of Commercial Street and Dock Street in Leith are also worth a visit.

Edinburgh Crystal in Penicuik – free shuttle bus from Waverley Bridge – has an array of crystal articles on sale in its factory shop.

In the Royal Mile there are gourmet food shops selling smoked salmon, kippers, cheese, haggis, oatcakes, shortbread and Dundee cake as well as malt whisky.

■ Entertainment ■

What's On, a monthly magazine, lists films, plays and concerts on offer in town. Hotels hold "Scottish Evenings" including traditional fare and entertainment and pubs like the Ensign Ewart in Lawnmarket and the Car Wash in North Bank Street organise jazz or folk events.

Night-clubs

Edinburgh has a lively club scene, with venues coming into and going out of fashion all the time. There is a bewildering variety of specials and one-nighters going on at any one time, so pick up *The List* and keep your eyes open for flyers in trendy bars and music shops such as **Underground Solushun**, on Cockburn Street. As well as the clubs listed above, tried and tested include **The Vaults** on Niddry Street, **Club Mercado** on Market Street and **Po Na Na** on Frederick Street. Leith is presently a boom area for clubbing. All city clubs close at 3am.

Comedy

The Fringe is the place to catch the best comedians in Britain but at other times of the year the top venue is **The Stand**, on York Place, with lots of laughs every night and a free Sunday lunch time session.

Theatre

As with comedy, August is the time to see la crème de la crème but throughout the year Edinburgh hosts plenty of top quality stuff. **The Traverse Theatre** (new writing; on Cambridge Street ☎ 0131 228 1404), the **Edinburgh Playhouse** (touring West End musicals), the **Royal Lyceum** (Grindlay Street, off Lothian Road ☎ 0131 248 4848) and the **King's Theatre** (other popular productions; 2 Leven Street ☎ 0131 529 600) are the main venues. The latter is an Edwardian gem, worth the ticket price alone to enjoy its lavish interior. In keeping with the city's Fringe tradition, there are also several smaller venues.

Cinema

The home of the **International Film Festival** in August is **The Filmhouse**, on Lothian Road, so cineastes are sure of a warm welcome year round. **The Lumiere**, at the Royal Museum, and **The Cameo** on Home Street are other favourites for cult and art-house movies. Otherwise there are lots of multiplexes to choose from.

Scottish Evenings

If the idea of a Scottish feast, bagpipes, Highland dancing and other such entertainment appeals, there are two Scottish Evenings in city centre hotels: **George Scottish Evening** at the George Intercontinental (May-early Oct; ☎ 0131 225 1251); and **Hail Caledonia** at the Carlton (May-mid Sept; ☎ 0131 472 3000).

For all the above forms of entertainment, buy a copy of *The List* from any newsagent to see who's on and forthcoming, or pick up a copy of the monthly magazine *What's On* at the Edinburgh and Lothians Tourist Board office.

CHILDREN

While the great architecture, galleries, historical buildings, museums and pubs of the city are mostly for adults, there are plenty of activities for kids too.

Princes Street Gardens are a good place to let off steam, particularly at the west end where there is a good playground. So too is the **Royal Botanic Garden** but for the real outdoors go to **Holyrood Park**.

On the Royal Mile, try the **Camera Obscura**, the **Museum of Childhood**, watch fudge being made next door, then nip down **Chalmer's Close** opposite to do some brass rubbing. At the foot of the Mile, **Dynamic Earth** is great for all the family.

There are several options just out of the centre. A boat trip on *The Maid of the Forth* to **Inchcolm Island**; its little beach and seal spotting are winners on a warm day. **Butterfly and Insect World** and the **Birds of Prey Centre**, at Lasswade, are deservedly popular, and will be even better when the new £2 million pyramid glasshouse, with lush rainforest and exotic inhabitants, is complete. Two other tried and trusted major attractions are **Deep Sea World** and **Edinburgh Zoo**.

On the ghost theme, try Witchery Tours (☎ 0131 225 6745) for a gentle fright; hard-boiled teens will enjoy the Edinburgh Dungeon and the City of the Dead Tour.

June is a particularly good time to visit, when the **Scottish International Children's Festival** (theatre, film, music, art and dance events) takes place. For events and activities year-round, see the Kids page in *The List*.

■ Where to Stay and Where to Eat ■

Pubs

The best way to sample the local brews is on a pub crawl starting at the **Abbotsford** in Rose Street or the **Café Royal**, the haunt of literary celebrities, in Register Place. The latter boasts an oyster bar. **Deacon Brodie's** in Lawnmarket or **Greyfriars Bobby** in Candlemaker Row are also fine establishments. There are pubs with a lively atmosphere popular with students in Grassmarket, and fashionable pubs and wine bars by the riverside in Leith. These establishments all offer simple meals at reasonable prices.

Restaurants

Edinburgh has a wide range of restaurants; those offering Scottish fare are identified by the Taste of Scotland logo.

The two prices given for each establishment represent a minimum and maximum price for a full meal excluding beverages.

Off The Wall, 105 High St, EH1 1SG; ☎ 0131 558 1497; otwedinburgh@aol.com; £15-£39. Located on the Royal Mile, though hidden on first floor away from bustling crowds. Vividly coloured dining room. Modern menus underpinned by a seasonal Scottish base.

Duck's at Le Marche Noir, 2-4 Eyre Pl, EH3 5EP; ☎ 0131 558 1608; bookings@ducks.co.uk; £21.65-£35.60. Confident, inventive cuisine with a modern, discreetly French character, served with friendly efficiency in bistro-style surroundings – intimate and very personally run.

The Marque, 19-21 Causewayside, EH9 1QF; ☎ 0131 466 6660; £11.50-£31.00. Arresting yellow decor and modern art won't distract attention from an original menu and smart service. A good lunch or pre-theatre choice; expect subtle Provençal touches.

Channings, 12-16 South Learmonth Gdns, EH4 1EZ; ☎ 0131 315 2225; £16-£46. Choose between rich traditional warmth or a chic, Scandinavian-inspired conservatory and enjoy a well thought-out range of characterful dishes, some with Italian overtones.

Martins, 70 Rose St, North Lane, EH2 3DX; ☎ 0131 225 3106; martinirons@fsbdial.co.uk; £19-£37. A concise menu of tasty, well-prepared options from local, mostly organic produce behind an unprepossessing façade. An impressive cheeseboard.

Hadrian's, 2 North Bridge, EH1 1TR; ☎ 0131 557 5000; £11-£24.75. Drawing on light, clean-lined styling, reminiscent of Art Deco, and a "British new wave" approach; an extensive range of contemporary brasserie classics and smart service.

Rogue, 67 Morrison St, EH3 8HH; ☎ 0131 228 2700; info@rogues-uk.com; £13-£36. Stylish, bright venue with beautiful wooden stripped bar. Contemporary feel: chrome and leather chairs and covered tables. Modern international menu includes grill section.

Marque Central, 30b Grindley St, EH3 9AX; ☎ 0131 229 9859; £12.50-£28.40. Generous, reasonably priced dishes which draw on contemporary Scottish and Italian traditions with equal facility. A popular modern restaurant near the Old Town.

Yumi, 2 West Coates, EH12 5JQ; ☎ 0131 337 2173. £25-£45. Comprehensive Japanese dining experience: authentically prepared cuisine comes into its own, thanks to charming, attentive staff and a number of well-structured set menus.

The Tower Museum of Scotland (fifth floor), Chambers St, EH1 1JF; ☎ 0131 225 3003; mail@tower-restaurant.com; £18.40-£42.85. Game, grills and seafood feature in a popular, contemporary brasserie style menu. On the fifth floor of the Museum of Scotland – ask for a terrace table and admire the view.

La Garrigue, 31 Jeffrey St, EH1 1DH; ☎ 0131 557 3032; jeanmichel@lagarrigue.co.uk; £14.70-£21.50. Very pleasant restaurant near main railway station: beautiful handmade wood tables add warmth to rustic décor. French regional cooking with classical touches.

Iggs, 15 Jeffrey St, EH1 1DR; ☎ 0131 557 8184; iggisbarioja@aol.com; £14.50-£31.25. Just off the Royal Mile, a comfortable, friendly restaurant overseen by the owner. Dishes are tasty, Spanish-influenced and of generous proportions.

Hurricane, 45 North Castle St, EH2 3BJ; ☎ 0131 226 0770; info@hurricanerestaurants.com; £17.90-£33.90. Bright and breezy restaurant in the city centre, enhanced by busy basement bar and colourful modern artwork. Good value menus of a hearty and robust nature.

Bouzy Rouge, I Alva St, EH2 4PH, ☎ 0131 225 9594; res@bouzy-rouge.com; £14.95-£26.50. An interior in bold blues and reds; tiles and flagged floors make for a slightly Mediterranean ambience. Modern British menu with a few eclectic variations. All day dining.

Nargile. 73 Hanover St, EH2 IEE, ☎ 0131 225 5755; £15.95-£24.70. Unpretentious and welcoming restaurant with simple décor and enthusiastic service. A la carte, set menus and lunch time mezes of tasty, well-prepared Turkish cuisine.

Le Café Saint-Honoré, 34 North West Thistle Street Lane, EH2 IEA, ☎ 0131 226 2211; £27.90-£30.75. Tucked away off Frederick St., a bustling, personally run bistro furnished in the classic French style of a century ago. Good-value cuisine with a pronounced Gallic flavour.

Blue, 10 Cambridge St, EH1 2ED, ☎ 0131 221 1222; £14-£25.65. Strikes a modern note with bright, curving walls, glass and simple settings. A café-bar with a light, concise and affordable menu drawing a young clientele. Bustling feel.

Hotels

The two rates quoted for each establishment refer to the nightly rate of a single or double room. Breakfast may not always be included in the price.

The Lodge, 6 Hampton Terr, West Coates, EH12 5JD; ☎ 0131 337 3682; re servations@thelodgehotel.co.uk; £65-£120. A converted Georgian manse, family owned and immaculately kept. Individually designed bedrooms and lounge decorated with taste and care; close to Murrayfield rugby stadium.

Kildonan Lodge, 27 Craigmillar Park, EH16 5PE; ☎ 0131 667 2793; info@kildonanlodgehotel.co.uk; £55-£138. Privately managed, with a cosy, firelit drawing room which feels true to the Lodge's origins as a 19C family house. One room has a four-poster bed and a fine bay window. Classical dining room; parquet floor spread with rugs.

Travel Inn Metro, I Morrison Link, EH3 8DN; ☎ 0131 228 9819; £50. Large hotel provides a consistent standard of modern budget accommodation. Between the conference centre and Haymarket station – a real plus for business travellers.

17 Abercromby Place, 17 Abercromby Pl, EH3 6LB; ☎ 0131 557 8036; eirlys.lloyd@virgin.net; £70-£100. Once home to architect William Playfair. Bedrooms – some overlooking wooded gardens – are furnished with character and attention to detail. Cosy library to rear.

19 St Bernard's Crescent, 19 St Bernard's Crescent, EH4 INR; ☎ 0131 332 6162; balfourwm@aol.com; £80-£115. Grand Doric pillars frame the entrance to this charming Georgian town house. An air of historical grandeur permeates the antique furnished communal rooms and bedrooms.

Seven Danube Street, 7 Danube St, EH4 1NN; ☎ 0131 332 2755; sev en.danubestreet@virgin.net; £70-£125. Bright, traditionally styled rooms with antique furnishings in a residential street. Breakfasts taken around one large table add to a feeling of engaging hospitality.

16 Lynedoch Place, 16 Lynedoch Pl, EH3 7PY; ☎ 0131 225 5507; susie.l ynedoch@btinternet.com; £50-£100. Under charming family management for over 20 years, a listed Georgian residence close to the West End with cosy and well maintained en suite rooms.

22 Murrayfield Gardens, 22 Murrayfield Gdns, EH12 6DF; ☎ 0131 337 3569; mac@number22.co.uk; £45-£80. Inviting fireside sofas and light, comfortable accommodation in a handsome Victorian house, managed with enthusiasm and care. Ideally located for Murrayfield Stadium.

The Stuarts, 17 Glengyle Terr, EH3 9LN; ☎ 0131 229 9559; red@the-stuarts.com; £65-£95. Each room in this smartly kept guest house boasts a contemporary look and an impressive range of modern conveniences. Faces a 36-hole short golf course.

Kew House, 1 Kew Terr, Murrayfield, EH12 5JE; ☎ 0131 313 0700; info@kewhouse.com; £60-£120. Secure private parking and good road access for the city or Murrayfield Stadium. Neat, carefully kept rooms which are modern and well-proportioned.

Newington Cottage, 15 Blacket Pl, EH9 1RJ; ☎ 0131 668 1935; fmickel @newcot.demon.co.uk; £70-£110. Substantial 19C villa in quiet residential area. Filled with much period charm: antiques, fresh flowers and curios. Well appointed rooms: decanter of sherry awaits on arrival.

LEITH

Express by Holiday Inn, Britannia Way, Ocean Drive, Leith, EH6 6JJ; ☎ 0131 555 4422; info@hiex-edinburgh.com; £99. Modern, purpose-built hotel offering trim, bright, reasonably-priced accommodation. Convenient for Leith centre restaurants and a short walk from the Ocean Terminal.

Camping

The nearest official site to the city centre is at Silverknowes (Marine Drive ☎ 0131 312 6874) 5 km (3 1/2 miles) northwest of the city. There is a direct bus service into town from outside the camp site. Contact the Tourist Information Office for other sites.

Language

Although it has many words and sayings of its own, Scottish is basically a dialect of the English language. The Edinburgh accent is much softer and more intelligible to visitors than that of other parts of Scotland. Here are a few Scottish words that you may encounter:

auld	old (the Auld Alliance is with the French; the Auld Enemy generally refers to England!)
bonnie	pretty, beautiful
burn	stream
ceilidh	(pronounced *caley*) gathering for Scots/Gaelic singing, dancing and story-telling
clan	family or Highland tribe
couthy	nice, pleasant
douce	mild, gentle, kind (also used of pleasant weather)
dram	measure (of whisky)
dreich	(pronounced *dreech*, with a hard *ch*) dull, wet, miserable, of weather
glen	Highland valley
ken	know (as in, d'ye ken...?/ do you know.....?)
kirk	church
laird	lord
laddie	boy
lassie	girl
Sassenach	non-Scot (usually perjorative, of English people)
see you!	Hey! (to attract attention)
wee	small
wynd	narrow alleyway between houses

■ Further reading ■

A Century of the Scottish People 1560-1830 – T C Smout, Fontana Press 1987

Capital of the Mind: How Edinburgh Changed the World – James Buchan 2003

The Scottish Enlightenment: The Scots' Invention of the Modern World – Arthur Herman, Fourth Estate 2003

The Edinburgh History of Scotland: 1689 to the Present – William Ferguson, Mercat 1995

The Story of Scotland – Nigel Tranter, Lochar Publishing Ltd 1991

Scotland, A New History – Michael Lynch, Pimlico 1992

A Concise History of Scotland – Fitzroy Maclean, Thames & Hudson 2000

The Battle for Scotland – Andrew Marr, Penguin 1995

Scottish Painting 1837 to the Present – William Hardie, Studio Vista 1990

Scottish Art 1460-1990 – Duncan Macmillan, Mainstream Publishing Company (Edinburgh) 1990

Poetical Works of Robert Burns edited by W & R Chambers Ltd 1990

Reflections on Scotland – Ian Wallace, Jarrold Colour Publications 1988

Scotland, An Anthology – Douglas Dunn, Fontana 1992

Whisky Galore – Compton Mackenzie, Penguin Books 1957

Broths to Bannocks – Catherine Brown, John Murray Ltd 1990

■ Calendar of Events ■

January 25th **Burns Night**: Burns Night Haggis, neeps, tatties and whisky are consumed in pubs and restaurants, while a piper plays and the poems of Burns are puzzled over by confused visitors on this, the occasion of the Bard of Scotland's birthday.

April **Edinburgh International Science Festival:** Events and lectures on a wide range of subjects are held throughout the city, with more hands-on events for the children.

April 30 **Beltane:** This ancient ritual of seasonal rebirth was reborn on Calton Hill in 1988 and has been going strong ever since, with lots of drumming, fires and dressing up. The starring roles go to the May Queen and the Green Man.

May **Scottish International Children's Festival:** The turn of the youngsters to enjoy Edinburgh's propensity for a good festival, with performing arts, magic, mime and puppet shows.

May, third Monday **Victoria Day** (Edinburgh only): Bank Holiday

June, third week **Royal Highland Show:** The highlight of Scotland's country calendar, featuring all things rural – food, livestock, flowers, crafts and more.

Last week in July, first week in August **Jazz and Blues Festival:** First class j 'n' b percolates from the city's smokiest dives to its smartest theatres, out into the fresh air of Princes Street Gardens, and also Grassmarket, where a mini Carnival takes place.

July-August **Edinburgh Book Fair:** Takes place every two years (2003, 2005…)

August	Edinburgh Festival **Edinburgh International Festival**; **Military Tattoo**; **The Fringe**; **Folk Festival**; **Jazz Festival**: The mainstream International Festival, the Military Tattoo and The Fringe last for three weeks, the Film Festival and the Book Festival last two weeks. A fantastic Firework Concert takes place in Princes Street Gardens on the last Saturday of the Festival.
September; third Monday	Autumn Holiday (Edinburgh only): Bank Holiday
September (usually over a weekend at the end of the month)	**Open Doors Day:** Take a look behind closed doors as some of the finest historical and architecturally interesting private houses and buildings in Edinburgh are opened to the public.
29 December– 2 January	**Hogmanay:** The Scots take New Year's Eve (Hogmanay) seriously – so seriously, in fact, that it is now Europe's biggest winter festival and is spread over five days to dilute its excesses. It includes street parties, fireworks and processions with firebrands; the burning of a Viking-style longboat is a recent addition. Beware that some pubs close early on New Year's Eve so that publicans can celebrate at their own private parties. Also, because of the crush in the city centre, note that you are not allowed into the most central area without a ticket which you must obtain in advance.

INDEX

Places and sights
People, historical events and subjects

A

Adam, Robert................ 14, 49, 55
Anne of Denmark, Queen 40
Argyll, Archibald Campbell,
  8th Earl of....................................41
Arthur's Seat..................................37
Assembly Rooms..........................56

B

Bailie MacMorran's House 40
Beltane Fire Festival 66
Black Dinner 26
Bonnie Prince Charlie..................26
Bonnie Prince Charlie..................35
Brass Rubbing Centre..................44
Bruce, Sir William................ 35, 36
Buchan, Earls of............................58
Buchan House............................ 58
Burns, Robert 40, 67

C

Café Royal 58
Calton Hill 66
Camera Obscura, Edinburgh 39
Canongate Church 44
Canongate Tolbooth 44
Canongate......................................44
Car Hire..80
Carlyle, Thomas 15
Car Rental 80
Castlelaw Hill Fort.......................75
Castle Rock...........................8, 26
Charles II.......................................35

C (continued)

Charles I....................................9, 34
Charlotte Square..........................55
City Chambers 43
Committee Chambers.................43
Corstorphine Hill.........................71
Covenanters......................9, 41, 46
Cowgate...46
Craig, James 54
Craigmillar Castle 74
Cruickshank, Helen......................15
Culloden, Battle of.......................35

D

Darien Scheme 9
Darnley, Henry Stewart, Lord ...37
David I 8, 34
David II 26, 37
Davies, Sir Peter Maxwell...........16
Dean Gallery.................................70
Douglas, Bishop Gavin 8
Duddingston..................................37
Dunbar, Battle of 9
Dunbar, William 8
Dundas, Henry, Viscount
  Melville..58
Dundas House................................58
Dunsterfield, George....................36
Dyce, William 18
Dynamic Earth...............................45

E

Edinburgh Castle..........................26
Edinburgh Experience 67

Edinburgh International
  Festival 16
Edinburgh Zoo.............................71
Encyclopaedia Britannica............43
Episcopacy 9, 40

F

Faed Brothers 18
Film Festival..................................16
Flodden Field, Battle of 8, 34
Flodden Wall 8, 47
Folk Festival..................................16
Food..22
Fringe, The 16

G

General Assembly Hall...............39
General Post Office.....................59
General Register House.............59
George Heriot's School..............47
George IV 35
George Street...............................56
Georgian House...........................56
Gladstone's Land..........................40
Glasgow School............................16
Graham, James Gillespie..... 15, 39
Grassmarket.................................46
Gregory, James,
  the Astronomer.........................74
Greyfriars Church and
  Churchyard...............................46
Gunn, Neil.....................................15

H

Halbert, John 36
Hamilton, Gavin 17
Heart of Midlothian.....................43
Heriot George
  (Jinglin Geordie) 9, 47

Hillend Ski Centre 75
Hogg, James 'The Ettrick
  Shepherd' 15
Holyroodhouse Abbey
  and Palace 34
Holyrood Park...............................37
Honours of Scotland...................33
Hub, The...39
Hume, David......................... 14, 58
Huntly House.................................45
Hutton, James................................14

J

Jacobite Rebellions......................... 9
James II 26, 34, 37
James III 26
James IV........................... 33, 34, 35
Jamesone, George.........................44
James V 37
James VI 40
James VI and I................................. 9
James VII and II.............................34
Jazz Festival....................................16
John Knox House 44

K - L

Kemp, George Meikle 60
Kirkcaldy of Grange,
  Sir William...................................26
Kirk o'Field............................ 37, 49
Knox, John 40, 41, 44
Lady Stair's House 40
Landseer,
  Sir Edwin 18
Lauderdale Family 36
Lauriston Castle 72
Law, John 72
Linlithgow......................................42
Lorimer, Sir Robert 31, 41

M

MacDiarmid, Hugh 15
Mackenzie, Henry.........................15
Makars, The.................................. 8
Malcolm III (Canmore) 8
Malleny Garden 75
Margaret, Queen 8, 31
Marston Moor, Battle of..............9
Mary, Queen
  of Scots.....................8, 35, 37, 74
McCullough, Horatio...................17
McTaggart, William 19
Military Tattoo 16, 26
Millais, John Everett 19
Mons Meg.....................................30
Montrose, Marquess of...9, 41, 42
Moray House 44
Moray, James Stewart,
  Earl of...42
Moray, Regent 42
More, Jacob....................................17
Morton, James Douglas,
  Regent...26
Mowbray House............................44
Muir, Edwin 15
Museum of Childhood................44
Mylne, John 43, 44
Mylne, Robert 35, 47
Mylne's Court 39

N - O

Nasmyth, Alexander.....................17
National
  Covenant 9, 41, 45, 46
National Gallery
  of Scotland....................................61
National Monument 66
Nelson Monument........................66
New Register House 58

New Town....................................54
North, Christopher 15
Observatory..................................66
Old University 49
Outlook Tower and Camera
  Obscura..39

P

Paolozzi, Eduardo 71
Parliament Hall 43
Paton, Noel............................ 18, 42
People's Story Museum 44
Perth 19
Phillip, John Spanish.....................18
Philliphaugh, Battle of 9
Playfair, William 15, 49, 65, 67
Princes Gardens 60
Princes Street................................60

R

Raeburn, Henry 15, 17
Ramsay, Allan (Jnr)......................17
Ramsay, Allan (Snr)........ 14, 18, 38
Ramsay Lodge 38
Reformation, The....................8, 40
Regalia (Honours
  of Scotland) 33
Reid, Robert 15
Riddle's Court................................40
Rizzio, David 37, 74
Rothesay, Robert, Duke of.........41
Rough Wooing 8
Royal Botanic Garden.................68
Royal Mile 38
Royal Museum of Scotland 50
Royal Observatory 74
Royal Scots Regimental
  Museum 29
Royal Scottish Academy 65
Royal Yacht Britannia..................69

S - T

St Andrew and
St George Church 57
St Andrew's House 66
St Andrew Square 58
St Giles' Cathedral......................40
St Mary's Episcopal Cathedral...69
Scotch Whisky Heritage
Centre 38
Scottish Agricultural Museum ...73
Scottish Colourists......................70
Scottish National Gallery
of Modern Art 70
Scottish National Portrait
Gallery...57
Scottish Parliament
Visitor Centre...........................43
Scottish Parliament......................39
Scottish Renaissance 15
Scott Monument 60
Scott, Sir
Walter............. 15, 17, 33, 40, 56
Smith, Adam.......................... 14, 45
Solemn League and Covenant..... 9

Spence, Lewis 15
Stevenson, R L 40, 42, 59
Stewart, Dugald 14, 67
Stone of Destiny (Scone)...........33
Strachan, Douglas.......................41
Stuart, Charles Edward....... 26, 35
Talbot Rice Gallery......................49
Treaty of Union 44
Tron Kirk 44

U - V

Union of Parliaments 33
Union of the Crowns................... 9
Scottish United
Services Museum 31
University of Edinburgh.............48
Victoria, Queen 35

W - Z

Wet, Jacob de...............................36
Whisky.................................... 23, 39
Wilkie, David.................................17
Wilkie, Sir David 36
Writers' Museum..........................40
Zoo..71

Director	David Brabis
Series Editor	Mike Brammer
Editorial	Alison Hughes
Picture Editor	Eliane Bailly, Geneviève Corbic
Mapping	Michèle Cana, Alain Baldet
Graphics Coordination	Marie-Pierre Renier
Graphics	Antoine Diemoz-Rosset
Lay-out	Michel Moulin, Alain Fossé
Typesetting	Sophie Rassel and Franck Malagie (NORDCOMPO)
Production	Renaud Leblanc
Marketing	Cécile Petiau, Hervé Binétruy
Sales	John Lewis (UK), Robin Bird (USA)
Public Relations	Gonzague de Jarnac, Paul Cordle

Contact	Michelin Travel Publications
	Hannay House
	39 Clarendon Road
	Watford
	Herts
	WD17 1JA
	United Kingdom
	☎ (01923) 205 240
	Fax (01923) 205 241
	www.ViaMichelin.com
	TheGreenGuide-uk@uk.michelin.com

Travel Publications

Hannay House, 39 Clarendon Road.
Watford, Herts WD17 IJA, UK
www.ViaMichelin.com
TheGreenGuide-uk@uk.michelin.com

. . . .

MANUFACTURE FRANÇAISE DES PNEUMATIQUES MICHELIN
Société en commandite par actions au capital de 304 000 000 EUR
Place des Carmes-Déchaux – 63 Clermont-Ferrand (France)
R.C.S. Clermont-Fd B 855 200 507

Published in 2004

Front cover:
The Old Town – Britannia – New Town – Whisky Tasting – West End Taxi – Edinburgh Castle
(All courtesy Edinburgh and Lothian Tourist Board)